THE PROPHET OF
THE DEAD SEA SCROLLS

The Essenes and the Early Christians —
One and the Same Holy People.
Their Seven Devout Practices

Also by Upton Clary Ewing: *The Essene Christ*

About the Author

Dr. Upton Clary Ewing was a theologian whose freedom from traditional commitments afforded him wider vistas of thought and broader means of religious expression. The story of his life and works is amazing. He was master of several arts, an award-winning architect, a sculptor and a painter of note, an inventor having many firsts to his credit, and an author who wrote and lectured on various philosophical, ethical, scientific, and religious subjects. It is understandable why Pulitzer Prize winner Dr. Albert Schweitzer referred to him as the "the renaissance of Leonardo da Vinci."

THE PROPHET OF
THE DEAD SEA SCROLLS

The Essenes and the Early Christians —
One and the Same Holy People.
Their Seven Devout Practices

Upton Clary Ewing

Tree of Life Publications

Tree of Life Publications, P. O. Box 126
Joshua Tree, CA 92252

A new edition, with a new foreword, cover, and editing.

Library of Congress Cataloging-in Publication Data

Ewing, Upton Clary.
    The prophet of the Dead Sea scrolls / by Upton Clary Ewing
        p. cm.
    Previously published: New York: Philosophical Library, 1963.
    Includes bibliographical references and index. Editing and
    new foreword by Bianca Leonardo.
    ISBN: 0-930852-24-9
1. Dead Sea scrolls—Criticism, interpretation, etc. 2. Teacher of
Righteousness. 3. Dead Sea scrolls—Relation to the New
Testament.
I. Title
BM487.E9   1993
296.8'1—dc20   93-16506
                                          CIP

CHARGE ORDERS: (800) 200-2046
BOOKLISTS AVAILABLE
FAX: 760-366-3596; PHONE: 366-3695

DEDICATED

To the ancient Essenes, and to
spiritual vegetarians in all ages,
everywhere.

CONTENTS

Chapter

FOREWORD
To this New Edition

Books on the Dead Sea Scrolls abound, but few touch upon this vitally important topic—the lifestyle of the ancient people, the devout Essenes, that included a bloodless, vegetarian diet.

Killing, roasting, and devouring animals took place in the temples at that time, in the guise of religious ceremonies. It was precisely this practice in the temples of Jerusalem that so offended Jesus, that he whipped the money changers out of the temple, and charged them: "How dare you make my Father's house a house of merchandise?"

Not only were doves bought and sold, but animals of all kinds and sizes—killed on the spot, then roasted and eaten voraciously by the priests and their followers. The altars were covered with blood and corpses, and the air filled with the screaming of slaughtered animals. Early Christian Fathers called this custom "diabolical."

Later, this practice was taken out of the temples and carried on in slaughterhouses, made secular, removed from religious ceremonies, and out of sight of the flesh eaters. And that is precisely what we have today, worldwide.

It is nothing short of **a world tragedy** that 2,000 years ago, the scribes and Pharisees so loved their **flesh feasts** that they deleted passages, garbled and interpolated the Holy Scriptures.

These same corrupted texts are with us today, and considered by most Christians to be the complete and true Scriptures. Their churches do not teach them otherwise. Flesh eaters believe (if they think about it at all), that animals were placed on earth solely for man's consumption. The truth of the matter is that **they have their own reason for existence.** The vast plant world, with its infinite variety, was provided for mankind's diet, and is totally adequate for health and the pleasure in eating.

In Genesis 1:29, mankind's true, pure, God-ordained diet is described. "God said, Behold, I have given you every herb-bearing seed, which is upon the face of all the earth, and every tree, in which is the fruit of a tree yielding seed; to you it shall be for meat (food)."

Today, that means all categories of fruits, vegetables, grains, nuts, seeds, and sea plants.

The slaughter of the animals continues today. In fact, it is worse than ever, with modern, international conglomerates operating in all countries. Not only are billions of animals cruelly slaughtered annually, worldwide, but the drugs and chemicals given them (for more and fatter profits), are killing people also,—with cancer and other diseases. The meat-centered diet of the West is also killing the planet—destroying the valuable rain forests, and polluting the waters and the soil.

We recommend reading this outstanding book, a 1987 Pulitzer prize candidate: *Diet for a New America*, by John Robbins. It is highly documented with facts every American should know. However, since the companies who breed animals for slaughter and consumption are international, and the sin of flesh-eating is worldwide, the book title *Diet for a New World* would be more appropriate. Yes, the breeding of animals for profit, for slaughter and consumption, is *a crime against the life force*, and mankind is suffering for this crime, in many ways. Ignorance is no excuse. Information on these subjects is plentifully available.

If the reader who is now a flesh eater will merely change his diet to a pure, vegetarian diet, and influence others to do the same, he or she will be doing much in the right direction. If one is a Christian, he would do well to have an open mind, and be willing to admit that much truth has been withheld throughout the ages. As we approach the twenty-first century, we must cast off old bondages of outdated beliefs, and rise into a new diet, a new health, a new and inspired life.

We must realize that it is mere commercialism that is handling us, molding our beliefs and thus our actions to the detriment of our highest good, our health, and the welfare of all the animals of the world, and ultimately the planet. Let us rise and free ourselves, and help our brothers and sisters who live in ignorance, help those who are trying to open the benighted eyes of large segments of mankind, and help our suffering planet. Only you can determine what you will put into your mouth and body. Multiplied, this change to a vegetarian diet will have a worldwide impact. Dear reader, please think on these things.

Bianca Leonardo, Editor

Bianca Leonardo is also an author and publisher, and was founder and president of a vegetarian society in Los Angeles, for fifteen years.

She is active in the Essene movement, as Reverend and Bishop of The Essene Foundation in San Diego, California. The latter honor was granted her since she studied with Prof. Edmond Bordeaux Szekely, Essene pioneer scholar and author. For further information on the The Essene Foundation, write to Tree of Life Publications, her company.

This Edition

The Prophet of the Dead Sea Scrolls was first published by the Philosophical Library, Publishers, in 1963. The new version has been given necessary editing, this foreword, a new cover, the Rembrandt etching, and the map.

Christ Driving Out the Money Changers, by Rembrandt

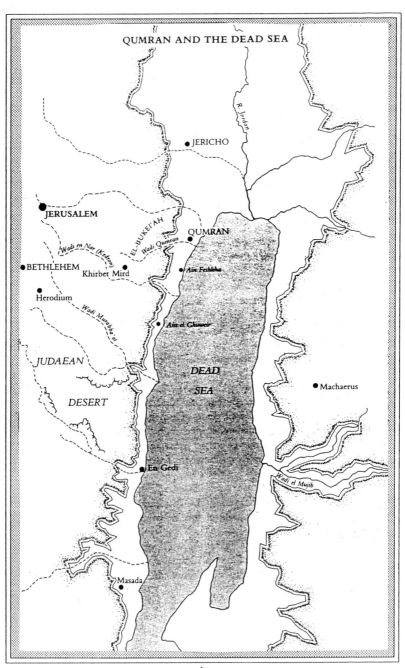

QUMRAN AND THE DEAD SEA

JERICHO

R. Jordan

JERUSALEM

QUMRAN

Wadi en Nar (Kedron)

EL-BUKEI'AH

Wadi Qumran

BETHLEHEM

Khirbet Mird

Ain Feshkha

Herodium

Wadi Murabba'at

Ain el Ghuweir

JUDAEAN

DEAD
SEA

Machaerus

DESERT

En Gedi

Wadi el Mujib

Masada

A map showing the Qumran area, where the Dead Sea Scrolls were found.

xiv

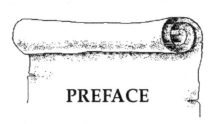

PREFACE

During the year of 1947, a most remarkable discovery of ancient manuscripts was made in a cave high up on a cliff overlooking the Dead Sea.

The people who placed them there for safekeeping, 2000 years ago, believed themselves to be the "Elect of God," the "Chosen Ones" whose purpose was to make the "highway straight in the desert for the coming of the Lord," as the prophet Isaiah had set forth in the Scriptures.

The unprejudiced scholarly evaluation of the contents of these old documents, referred to as the "Dead Sea Scrolls," has been the cause of no little interest, excitement, and concern among Bible scholars, theologians and laymen all over the world.

"It is quite true," writes Professor W. F. Albright, "that the discovery of the Scrolls menaces the insecure foundation of many speculative hypotheses of both Old and New Testament scholars, not to mention students of rabbinics. The new evidence with regard to the beliefs and practices of Jewish sectarians of the last two centuries B. C. bids fair to revolutionize our approach to the beginnings of Christianity." [1]

In fact, there is almost unanimity among scholars that the Jewish Sect of the Covenant "directly and immediately prepared the way for the Christian church, and that it helped to shape both the church's soul and its body." [2]

Nevertheless, there are those who oppose particularly the extremities of this point of view, and while admitting the uniqueness of the many parallels, lay particular stress upon the several non-conforming references found in the New Testament writings which confuse or favor an element of doubt.

Therefore, it is obvious if one is to recover a convincing picture of the sectarian background of Christianity, of the relationship between the Sect of the Scrolls and the Christian church, one must seek to find it not through endeavoring to make it conform exclusively to a Greco-Roman or New Testament frame of reference, but to view it as it actually existed as an heretical Jewish movement.

Thus one does not depend on the paralleling of scripture passages, for these merely supplement the basic issues which, as I shall point out, are the truly reliable means whereby **the Sect of the Scrolls and the followers of Jesus, called "The Christ," can be identified as the same people.**

But the information gained through the Scrolls is not in itself the complete evidence for the re-evaluation of Christian beginnings; there are many other bits of information which have been preserved by ancient writers. What the Scrolls have done is to give us premises upon which we can now verify the truth of other historical data concerning the origin of Christianity, and the ethical system of the immediate followers of Jesus.

The Hebrew sect called the Nazarenes, or Ebionites, in their search for truth, proclaimed evidence of great antiquity, which confirmed their faith and which challenged the validity of the Mosaic Law as it was interpreted by the temple priests.

Epiphanius, the celebrated scholar of the third century; wrote: "The Nazarenes held that the Jewish form of the Pentateuch was not that which Moses received but a later fabrication; the Nazarenes claimed that they possessed the true law."[3]*

Paralleling this report of Epiphanius about the Nazarenes, Dr. Theodore Gaster, after translating the Scrolls, wrote of the Essenes: "They were not waiting to receive the law—they already possessed it. Their aim was to deliver it from the realms of darkness in which it had been engulfed. The Torah, that is, the Divine Teachings as revealed to Moses—had, it was held, been successively perverted by false expositors." [4]*

Apparently, the Old Testament as we have it today, was condemned by the Essenes, Nazarenes, or first Christians.

The book of Deuteronomy (repetition of the law) was written by the priests of Jerusalem. It was the first book canonized about the year 600 B.C., or about the same time that the great reformer Jeremiah cried out: "The prophets prophesy falsely, and the priests rule at their direction. Trust ye not in lying words....How can you say 'We are wise and the law of the Lord is with us?' Behold, the false pen of the scribes has made it into a lie." (5:31, 7:4, 8:8).

Conforming with the protests of Jeremiah, the Essene scriptures say: "But for thy people lying priests flatter them, and deceitful scribes lead them astray. They have plotted wickedness, seeking to exchange thy holy engraven word for the smooth things they address to thy people, making them to turn their gaze into the errors they teach, revelling in their feasts, ensnaring themselves with lusts." [5]

An early century document describes the Apostle Peter as referring to many chapters of the Old Testament as having been interpolated by the devil. [6] Barnabas, the companion of St. Paul, said: "...the laws of the book of Leviticus are the work of a wicked angel." [7]

---

* Note that quotations 3 and 4 give evidence of a common identity between "The Sect of the Scrolls" and those called Nazarenes.

17

We note how others among the prophets, how Jesus (Mark 7:13) and the martyr Stephen spoke out against the false scribes and condemned the custom of animal sacrifice. **All of this tends to identify the Essenes, Nazarenes or early Christians as the same people.**

It is interesting to note that most of the opposition concerning the relationship of Christianity, and particularly Jesus, to the Sect of the Scrolls has come, in the past, through orthodox sources. However, in view of the later research exposing a formidable array of new data which, when categorized and orderly arranged, tells a story so convincing that one wonders how and upon what grounds these same sources can now justify their position. Indeed, it might be said that the leaders of the church are today in dire need of a convincing hypothesis which might tend to offset the critical position in which traditional Christianity is apparently placed through the discovery of the Scrolls.

For the past many centuries, Christian faith, in the story of Jesus, has withstood the many critical analyses of the gospel narratives. Scholars, scientists, explorers in the historical backgrounds of Bible lore, have set forth their findings, much of which leads to doubting the trustworthiness of the several New Testament reports concerning the historical Jesus.

However, Christian faith, in the significance of the gospel reports, has withstood the onslaughts of critical exegesis mainly because the uniqueness of the Christ story has resisted all attempts to produce a comprehensive historical facsimile of Jesus and his various activities and experiences.

But today, this position is no longer secure as witnessed in a later chapter of this work. Indeed, through a most revealing arranging of texts inclusive of the several "apocryphal" or "pseudepigraphic" writings found in the caves at Qumran, the uniqueness of the gospel Jesus is now clearly questioned. The eminent French scholar

Dupont-Sommer has pointed this out in his several writings on the Scrolls. He insists that the priority of the Christ story belongs to the Qumran Messiah who died about the year 65-63 B.C. [8]

However, there is a wide difference of opinion concerning the identity of the Qumran Teacher. The question therefore is, "did the Essene prophet actually exist as an historical character, or was he merely a shadowy figure idealized by Essene writers—one whose coming was looked forward to as the "Saviour of the world?"

Indeed, as the case now appears, it is upon a significant and plausible answer to this two-part question that the future security, or insecurity, of Christian theology depends. This statement may appear somewhat presumptuous but the reader will no doubt find, as the story unfolds, that it is in keeping with the evidence.

Consider, then, the first part of the question. If the findings of Dupont-Sommer are generally accepted, whereby it can be shown that the "Essene Messiah" was truly an historical figure in Judaism, one who was conceived through the "handmaid of God," who was the "suffering servant" foretold in Isaiah, who was baptized by the "Holy Spirit" as the only begotten son, who spoke to God as to a father, whose disciples turned their backs upon him and denied him up and down, who was condemned to death, was crucified and rose again for the salvation of the world—in fact, one around whom a whole mystery of salvation was elaborately set forth in scripture written many years before the New Testament—then it is clear that the Christian position, regarding the historicity of the gospel reports of the "latter day" Jesus is quite embarrassing, to say the least. Indeed, as Dupont-Sommer infers, "the denial, even to the historical existence of Jesus,—will at last find a clear and positive explanation." [9]

Now, as to the second part of the question, if it can be shown that the "Essene Teacher" was not, with any degree of certainty, an historical figure (which is what this writer proposes to do), then, indeed, Qumran references to this "Saviour, God and man," can be assigned to prophecy, in which case the uniqueness of the Christ story becomes unassailable. But such a tremendous strengthening of the Christian position must apparently be sustained through a recognition of the "Sect of the Scrolls" as "Christians before Jesus"—those who prophesied and anticipated the advent of the Christ, a viewpoint held by apologists and historians of the early church.

However, the accepting of Jesus as an Essene involves certain ethical implications which nascent Christianity has resisted down through the centuries. On the other hand, such acceptance would probably tend to revive the long obscured moral fibre of primitive Christianity which, in effect, should not particularly embarrass the worldly attitudes of churchmen, especially since the great soul-edifying doctrine of non-violence, as it was both practiced and preached by Jesus, has been completely ignored by the militant church for over sixteen centuries.

Therefore, it appears that the Church, at least in its efforts to gain favor in the Eastern world, would do well to strengthen its ethical foundation, if not its practices. This seems to be a small price to pay (accepting Jesus as an Essene) in view of the fact that the alternative clearly disputes the trustworthiness of the gospel reports, if not the very existence of the traditional Jesus.

Apparently, the reluctance among orthodox churchmen to recognize the Essene brethren as the first Christians before Jesus and therefore as inclusive of him, is based upon a "wait and see policy" rather than one precedented by early Church leaders.

The prominent apologist, St. Epiphanius (360 A.D.), recognized the Essenes as the first Christians before the advent of the "Son of man," saying, "Christians were called Essenes before those who believed in Christ were called

Christians." [10]   And again, **Eusebius, the distinguished father of Church history (264-349), saw in the New Testament a comparable recapitulation of Essene scripture.** He wrote, "The writings of ancient men who were the founders of the sect referred to by Philo, may very well have been the gospels and epistles which were not yet written." [11]

Apparently, what Epiphanius infers is that the Son of Man was anticipated by the Essene Christians who recognized him as the Christ. In the same sense, Eusebius, in referring to the Essene scriptures as anticipating the yet-unwritten gospels and epistles, prefaces the remarks of Epiphanius which sustain the appearance of Christ as an "Essene-Christian" event. Even the traditions of the Catholic Carmelite Order identify the apostles of Jesus and the "Holy Mother" herself with the Essenes. [12]

However, criticism today would not particularly favor these references as convincing means of identification. They, therefore, must be supported by other more conclusive evidences of proof. These are to be recognized through the exposition of certain customs, practices and doctrines, which were held exclusively by the Sect of the Scrolls and the primitive Christians and not by any other religious sect in Palestine. Without exception, the many books, papers and other articles written about the Sect of the Dead Sea Scrolls have either overlooked or neglected to explore sufficiently in these fields, particularly when it can be shown that they contain the most convincing of all evidences of proof relating or identifying a common society with a singular people.

In later chapters of this book, the reader will find a comprehensive review of these several evidences of proof which provide little known but reliable answers to the question of identity. In fact, **the search for identity is the main objective of this writer. It is to prove beyond a reasonable margin of doubt that the sect called Essenes and the sect referred to as Nazarenes or primitive Christians were, in all intent and purpose, one and the same people;** also, that Jesus called "The Christ," was the key figure in evidencing this to be true.

In consequence, the writer hopes to ameliorate the position of the Christian religion, to remove the element of doubt pertaining to the historicity of the Gospel Jesus and to view him as a symbol of love in its highest and purest state, unalloyed and uncompromised by the dictates of custom and the moral and spiritual immaturity of a self-indulgent society.

In a concluding chapter, the events leading up to the condemning and the crucifixion of Jesus are reevaluated and found to compare more realistically with historical data concerning his intent and purpose than has heretofore been recognized. Here also, and at long last brought to light, is presented a surprising bit of historical evidence which, contrary to traditional opinion, lays the sole demand and responsibility for the execution of Jesus directly at the feet of imperial Rome, thereby clearing the Jews of any participation in the event.

This new information should go a long way toward healing old scars and avoiding new wounds, coming at a time when men of good will are brought to realize that all men are brothers under the sun—that even though the great stream of life has become polluted after its flow from the eternal source, it still can be made more pure as it passes by and continues on its course.

U. C. Ewing

PREFACE
References

[1] Albright, Professor W. F., *Postscript to Brownlee's Translation of the Dead Sea Manual of Discipline*, Bulletin of the American Schools of Oriental Research, 1951.

[2] Fritsch, Charles T., in reference to Dupont-Sommer, *The Qumran Community*, Macmillan Co., N.Y.

[3, 10] Black, Matthew, *The Scrolls and Christian Origins*, pp. 72, 73 in re: (Epiphanius in his *Ossaens*), Scribners, N.Y.

[4, 5] Gaster, Theodore, *The Dead Sea Scriptures*, Doubleday, N.Y.

[6] Larson, Martin A., *The Story of Christian Origins*, published by the author.

[7] Goodspeed, Edgar J., *Introduction to the Apostolic Fathers*, Harper, N.Y.

[8, 9] Dupont-Sommer, *The Dead Sea Scrolls*, Basil Blackwell, Oxford, Macmillan, N.Y.

[11, 12] *Encyclopedia Britannica*, 11th Ed. Vol XXVI, p. 793, Vol. V, p. 358.

*   *   *   *   *

Abbreviations:

B.C.   = Before Christ

CDC   = Cairo Document of the Covenant, an ancient text, now more commonly referred to as the Damascus Document or the Damascus Rule. The text was first discovered in Cairo about one hundred years ago; thus, the now used abbreviation C.D., i.e., Cairo: Damascus

C.E.   = Common Era. Bible scholars now use this term instead of "A.D."—*anno domini* (in the year of the Lord).

DSD   = Dead Sea Documents

DSS   = Dead Sea Scrolls

K.J.V.   = King James Version

R.S.V.   = Revised Standard Version

CHAPTER ONE

The Holy Ones of Qumran*

The Scrolls Stored for Safekeeping

In the first century B.C., during the reign of the Herodian kings, there came to flower among the Hebrews a sect which was unique above all others in the world.

Numbering more than four thousand men, they, together with their families and kin which must have exceeded over ten thousand in all, dwelt in closely knit communities in various cities and towns of Judea.

"Moral philosophy and ethics was their chief preoccupation and their conduct was regulated in accord with the laws which governed them. These they especially studied on the seventh day which they held holy, leaving off all work upon it and meeting in their synagogues where they worshipped. Here one of them would read the Scriptures, and another who was very learned would expound whatever was obscure, explaining most things in their time-honored fashion by means of symbols, metaphors or parables.

"They were taught piety, holiness, justice, knowledge of what is really good and evil, and of what is indifferent, and what ends to avoid, what to pursue—in short, love of God, of virtue and of men.

---

*Pronounced *koomrahn* (An Arabic name of uncertain meaning).

"No maker of warlike weapons can be found among them. Least of all were any slaves found among them, for they saw in slavery a violation of the laws of nature, which made all men free." [1]

They believed themselves to be the last of a remnant which had survived since the time of Moses. Into their keeping was given the true interpretation of the Law as it was first inscribed on the tablets of old. They held that the Law, as it was practiced by the Pharisees and the Sadducees, had been successively garbled by false scribes and lying priests, and that it was their sacred duty to lift it out of the realms of darkness into which it had been submerged.

They did not believe in, nor practice, animal sacrifice, for which reason they were barred from the temple. Sacrifice was a heathen or Baalish custom which did not belong to the worship services of the Jews. It was adopted and put into practice by the priests, contrary to the pleasure of God as voiced by the prophets. "Shall I come before Him with burnt offerings, with calves of a year old? He has shown thee, O man, what is good, and what the Lord requires of thee, but to do justly and to love mercy and to walk humbly with thy God." (Micah 6:6-8). "For I desired *mercy* instead of sacrifice,* the knowledge of God more than burnt offerings." (Hosea 6:6). This same call for mercy was attested to by their own scriptures which say: "Keep the commandments of the Lord, and show mercy toward all, not toward men only, but also toward the beasts." [2]

They believed that one would receive the truth of the voice of scripture only when he was completely attuned, or had received the inner enlightenment. "The acquisition of that light, however, was not attributed to any sudden spontaneous act of grace. Rather was it the result of man's own voluntary exercise of that power of discernment which

---

*The significance of this phrase as it is restated in Matt. 12:7 will be more clearly understood as the reader continues.

God placed in every creature at the moment of its creation. All things, it was affirmed, . . . had been endowed by God with sensate knowledge, though the choice of using or ignoring it had been left, in the case of man, to his individual will. If he heeded the gift, he achieved harmony with the eternal cosmic scheme and broke the trammels of his morality. Automatically he was embraced in the communion of eternal things; he became one with the great forces of the universe. . . ." [3]

In other words, they believed that all creatures being endowed by God with sensate knowledge were, even as man, part of the great cosmic plan. Illumination, therefore, came through achieving harmony with the whole of life, which in effect is becoming one with the universe and, or, one with the author of all life. [4]

"And such teachings bore fruit. Their lifelong purity, their recognition of a good providence alone, showed their love of God. Their love of virtue revealed itself in their indifference to money, worldly position, and pleasure. Their

---

[4] It is not at all surprising to find that this same mystery was attested to by Jesus. In a first century Papyrus discovered in 1903, at Oxyrhynchus, Egypt, Jesus addresses his Apostles: "Ye ask who are those that draw us to the kingdom in Heaven? . . . the fowls of the air, and all beasts that are upon the earth and even the fishes of the sea. These are they which shall draw you. Strive therefore to know yourselves . . . and ye shall know ye are in the city of God." Again this mystery appears in the Old Testament: "Ask now the beasts, and they shall tell thee; and the fowls of the air, and they shall tell thee; and the fishes of the sea shall declare unto thee. Who knoweth not in all these that the hand of the Lord hath wrought? In whose hand is the *soul* of every living creature and the breath of all mankind." (Job 12:7-10). "The earth and the sea is full of thy creatures . . . living things both great and small . . . when thou sendest forth thy Spirit they are created." (Psalms 104:24-30).

This same mystical relationship is today rationalized in Albert Schweitzer's ethic of "Reverence for Life."

love of man in their kindliness, their quality, and their fellowship passed all words."[5] "And their long life—many live above a hundred years by means of their regular course of life and the simplicity of their diet."[6]

"Living as they did, in colonies, they threw open their doors to any of their sect who came their way. They had a storehouse, common expenditures, common raiments, common food eaten at common meals.

"This was made possible by their practice of putting whatever they earned each day into a common fund, out of which they also supported the sick when they could not work. The aged among them were held with respect and honor and were considered as parents to the community.[7]

They believed that the time was not far off when all men would be held accountable for their sins. They preached a doctrine of repentance, through which one might avoid the inevitable consequences of his wrongdoings. Only through works of righteousness, of kindness, mercy, and reverence for all of God's creations could one be assured of life instead of death.

They indeed looked forward to the coming of a Prophet after Moses, a Teacher of Righteousness who would dwell among them and instruct them in the truth of the way to eternal life. They believed that through him the word of God would be made plain to all who were ready to receive it.

Toward this end, they endeavored to fulfill the prophecy of Isaiah: "Prepare ye the way. Make straight in the desert a highway for the coming of the Lord." (40:3).

Selecting a site in the desert country outside Jerusalem, of which the prophet had spoken, they prepared to construct a place of refuge from the evils of the world.

Gathering rocks of various sizes which were in great abundance, having fallen down from the cliffs above, they constructed on a plateau overlooking the blue waters of the Dead Sea, a house of meditation, prayer and study.

In accord with the prophet Habakkuk they built into it a watchtower commanding a view north toward the river Jordan. From here by day they scanned the length and breadth of the wilderness for the coming of the promised "One" and by night they searched the heavens for a sign to herald the great event.

To this desert retreat came those of a priestly calling. Unlike the lay members of the sect, they did not take wives. They believed that the spirit of fornication, dwelling in the flesh of all men, was particularly more alluring and seductive in the body of a woman. Therefore, all those who were chosen to prepare the "highway in the desert" for the coming of the Lord must, along with other abstinences held in common by the Brotherhood, "walk blamelessly, not straying after thoughts of guilty lust or after whoring eyes."[8]*

These particularly "chosen ones" whose life was dedicated to "preparing the way" spent much time contemplating the Law and the Prophets which they interpreted through becoming themselves examples of righteous conduct.

Through profound studies of the mysteries of life and creation, they became attuned to the "Will and the works of God" in nature, and were privileged to partake of the many health-giving secrets hidden therein. In consequence, they gained particular knowledge of certain roots and herbs from which they obtained various extracts and oils to heal the sick. Comparable to those of the brotherhood in Egypt whom Philo called the "Therapeutae," (attendants, viz., physicians or healers) they performed through the "will" and the abounding gifts of Providence many remarkable cures, even to the raising up of those who had taken on the appearance of death.**

----

*Compare Matt. 5:28.

**Compare with the many healings of Jesus and others, in our Bible.

There were also those among them who were particularly gifted in predicting the future. Records have come down to us of certain events that came to pass exactly as they had been foretold.[9]

But these remarkable men were also dedicated teachers who expounded the law and the prophets and who prepared to lead the services in their community synagogues.

Occasionally, mere boys of twelve years, who had been dedicated even from their mother's womb to walk in the ways of God, were taken in under the tutelage of the holy ones. Thus the monastery was also an *academe* where those of a priestly calling came to seek out the secrets of the kingdom of heaven. Those who abided by the strict discipline of the order were, upon attaining the age of thirty, duly qualified as priests or rabbis. Thereafter, they either remained as one of those chosen to prepare the highway in the desert for the coming of "the anointed one" or they returned to their home communities to teach in the synagogues.

But, alas, there came a time when the "Holy Ones" of the desert monastery were to suffer the trials of the unexpected in their search for the good and the true. Even now, as they were vigilantly preparing the way for the coming of the Lord, the shadow of the evil one had cast its blight over the land.

This all came to pass during the rise of Herod the Great who, by collecting the tribute, had won the favor of the Roman Cassius, and again, through bribery, had gained the favor of Antony.

After Jerusalem fell to his armed might in 37 B.C., Herod was made king of the Jews. When Herod conquered the city he plundered the temple and took captive Antigonus, the high priest. He carried off the royal armaments, spoiled the wealth of the people, and put men to the sword without mercy. He heaped together great quantities of silver and gold and sent it to Antony as a tribute of his loyalty.

Now when Antony had received Antigonus as a captive, he decided to behead him, as Herod had requested. The Jews were growing seditious out of hatred for Herod, and they continued to bear good will for Antigonus. By no means could they be forced to call Herod, whose Edomitic blood they detested, their king.

The news of Herod's depredations at Jerusalem spread rapidly to the various communities of Judea, where dwelt together the lay members of the Sect of the Scrolls.

It was probably during this particularly debased period in the history of Palestine that many of the devout departed to the hill country of Galilee. Like a voice out of the past may have come the word: "Those who stood firm escaped to the land of the north." [10] This might well have been the move that led to the founding of a community which later became known as Nazareth.*

After Herod had consolidated his ill-gotten gains he embarked upon an extensive building program. Among his projects was a winter pleasure palace which occupied a site along the banks of the Wadi Qelt, several miles south of the old city of Jericho.

Herein Roman guests of high rank, even Antony himself, were entertained in the most pleasurable fashion that the sensual nature of man can conceive.

But while Herod was a sumptuous entertainer, a man of taste, a cunning politician and an able administrator, he was also a violent crusader with the heart of a pirate.

The predacious lusts of his warrior spirit were not to be quelled by the victories of yesterday, for the din of battle, the smell of blood, the impulse to plunder and the will to dominate the vanquished, cried out within him to carry on.

---

*See definition of Nazareth in this book.

We find him now preparing for a decisive campaign against the Arabians. Upon the plains of the Jordan Valley he called together a formidable horde of fighting men. To the south in the desert wilderness of the Dead Sea, and in close proximity to Wadi Qumran,* Herod's finest practiced the strategies of battle in preparation of the conquest beyond the Jordan.

But the presence of these men of violence was indeed of grave concern to the elect among the brethren of Qumran who in their striving to attain the acme of spiritual success, had "kept themselves apart from any consort with froward men."

Indeed, the encroachment of these "Sons of darkness" upon the sanctity of their "Holy of holies" was viewed by the prophets among them as the sign of impending disaster. Thus, we attempt to reconstruct a picture of the state of affairs as they appear to have existed at Qumran leading up to the following events.

It is now 31 B.C. and in accord with the reports of the Jewish historian Josephus, an earthquake came upon the land, causing much destruction and a great loss of life. The King's fighting men on maneuver in the area were beset with fear and it took all the skill of their clever-tongued leader to embolden them to carry on. [11]

But now, what about the welfare of the brethren? Were the tolerances of providence more considerate of them? Apparently not, for their desert shelter suffered much damage. Great cracks appeared in the outer walls and in the steps extending down into the cistern, threatening the safety of their precious water supply.

Coincidentally, the first shock of the earthquake might have happened even while the brethren were at prayer bewailing the intrusion of the "Sons of Darkness" within the environs of their holy place. One can in consequence

---

* Even today, the Jordan Military Command finds the ruggedness of this area ideal for war games.

imagine the fearful reaction of this devout congregation as the very floors moved beneath their feet and the roof above their heads opened to the shafts of heaven. But almost as suddenly as it began the rumbling ceased and all was quiet again.

Recovering from their fears, the brethren huddled together, reasoning among themselves, saying: "Surely the prophecy cannot be fulfilled here and now, for the Lord has given us to know that his time is not yet." Thereupon a council was called to order and, as recent archeological evidence suggests, the decision was handed down to abandon the desert monastery.

Various groups of the brethren returned to their families or relatives residing in the several communities of Judea, while those of the inner circle who had been raised to the priesthood remembered the covenant which God had made with their forbears: "Those that keep the law shall be those who repent and depart from the land of Judea to sojourn in the land of Damascus." [12]

Thus, in accord with the word of scripture, a little band of pious souls set out on the long hazardous journey to Damascus.

And now after dramatizing the events leading up to the evacuation of Qumran, as evidenced both by historical record and through the findings made at the Dead Sea ruins,* suppose we look in upon this little band of courageous exiles whom we now find somewhere in the ancient city of Damascus.

*   *   *

It is now about the year 6-4 B.C. or about a quarter century since the surviving members of the Qumran priesthood had come out of the land of their fathers. Though

---

*Coins found in the ruins run in a continuous chain dating from 104 B.C. to 37 B.C. The series begins again dating from 4 B.C. and again to A.D. 68.

time had weighed heavily upon these faithful souls, they had not despaired. Being raised up as teachers, it was of their calling to instruct others. They very likely established a congregation of followers, many of whom were being made eligible to accompany the elect when the word was given to return to their "holy of holies."

Each night, as was their custom, several of the brethren kept watch, scanning the heavens with the hope of discovering some sort of sign which might inform them that the time was near for a return to the deserts of Judea: "To make straight there a highway for the coming of the Lord."

It was during these periods of watch that a most unusual phenomenon appeared in the night heavens. According to astronomers, a fiery conjunction of several planets[13] appeared in the zodiacal sign of Pisces. Strangely enough, from a calculated alignment with Damascus, Pisces appears south by southeast, or in the direction of both the Qumran monastery and a little town called Bethlehem. The question now is, did the elect, upon witnessing this phenomenon, return immediately to their homeland or did they linger for awhile to complete their work at Damascus?

An affirmative answer to the latter half of the above question appears to be more in line with the evidence, for according to the findings of archeologists excavating in the ruins*, the monastery could not have been reoccupied before the year 4 B.C.

However, according to astronomers, it was during the year 4 B.C. that "a comet produced a heavenly spectacle." [14] Also, in the after part of this same year there was an eclipse of the moon. Of this latter phenomenon, it is said to have occurred during the passing of the wicked king, Herod

---

* The next gap in the date of coins found in the ruins extended to the reign of Archelaus (4 B.C.—6 A.D.), which indicates the beginning of the second period of occupation.

the Great. This might truly have been the sign for which the exiles at Damascus had been waiting.

In any case, their return to the Dead Sea monastery did apparently approximate the death of Herod the Great, which indeed substantiates the theory of why they left in the first place. But there was also another event which in its particular relevance in time to others just mentioned, should indeed be of extraordinary interest to theological students.

According to Christian tradition, the date of the crucifixion was Friday, the 14th of Nisan (A.D. 29). Hippolytus (A.D. 200) writes that Christ suffered in his thirty-third year.[15] This places the birth of Jesus in the year 4 B.C., which event was closely preceded in time by a fiery conjunction of the planets. It was also the same year that a comet appeared in the night heavens and again the same year, probably the latter part, that an eclipse of the moon announced the passing of Herod the Great, and again, according to our evidence, the same year that the "chosen ones" returned to their desert sanctuary to prepare the way. ("Make straight a highway in the desert for the coming of the Lord.")

Of course, these various events, even though they coincide historically, are more interpretable theologically than they are on purely scientific grounds. Circumstantial evidence is not always conclusive, even when supported by facts and figures. On the other hand, error is less prevalent and facts and figures more consistent with truth when supported by the evidence of circumstances.

Be that as it may, the case in question is indeed intriguing, even if all the events pertaining to it are but strangely coincidental.

* * *

The time now is about 4 B.C., a time conforming both with a report that a babe was born in Bethlehem and with the evidence supporting the return of "The Wise Men" from the land east of the Jordan. No doubt the word went out at once to the brethren in Judea and Galilee of the return of the exiles from Damascus.

Soon eager hands were busy rebuilding walls, repairing roofs, constructing new water storage systems, restocking the library and in general making ready the holy place in the desert for the coming of the Lord.

Now this idea of preparing might have been more rational in scope than one might otherwise suppose. The men who founded the "Sect of the Scrolls" were highly intelligent beings. They were as conscientious in their mystical formulations as they were efficient in their economic planning. One might suppose that they purposely wrote into their scriptures certain cryptic words and phrases which they intended for the eyes of "One who was to come," that through his interpretation of these he would in due time make himself known and the prophesies be fulfilled. Now this idea does appear to be extremely hypothetical, but notwithstanding, and as we shall see later, it has quite revealing possibilities.

Returning again to the discussion of the various time periods wherein the brethren either occupied or evacuated the Qumran area, it has been proposed that their final departure occurred during the revolt of the Jews (68-70 A.D.).

Now, it is highly probable that the buildings at Qumran were in a limited degree inhabited from 4 B.C. until A.D. 68-70, but this does not necessarily mean that the doctrinal beliefs of the inhabitants or the inhabitants themselves did not undergo a state of change during this same period. Indeed, it is highly probable that a major change took place about the year 30 A.D. at which time, as certain rather pertinent evidences seem to suggest, the main seat of the brotherhood was transferred to Jerusalem. This was nearly forty years before the Roman occupation of the buildings at Qumran. In the meantime, a party of the brethren continued at the monastery, probably to maintain the place as a rest retreat and to look after the safekeeping of the many priceless manuscripts which had been collected over the years.

It has been said that the Scrolls were hurriedly stashed away just before the Romans stormed and burned the building. However, the evidence does not sustain this notion. The brethren did not gather up armsful of Scrolls and dash off to easy accessible hiding places. On the contrary, much time, thought and careful planning went into the project. Each scroll was carefully wrapped in linen and then given a coating of some sort of waxy substance. They were again put into stone jars provided with tight-fitting covers. These were sealed to further insure their preservation. Last, but not least, much planning and effort were given to the hiding away of these jars. They were carried, or hoisted up, high upon the walls of a cliff and put into small caves, the entrances of which were sealed with huge boulders.

It must be remembered that these hiding places were at the time a great more inaccessible than they are today. After centuries of erosion and the falling down of rubble from above, great banks have been built up which make for greater accessibility.

No doubt, charts marking the location of the caves were made, each cave numbered and its contents listed accordingly. This, of course, is supposition, but it must be considered as a logical conclusion.

Notwithstanding, however, the evidence does suggest that the Scrolls were not hurriedly hidden due to an emergency, but were stored for safekeeping under circumstances wherein fear was not the motive.

Accordingly, and as the evidence of circumstance becomes more convincing as we proceed, the year 30 A.D. or thereabouts, marks at least the partial evacuation of Qumran, and a relaxing, or a changeover in the customary rituals

---

See the Manual of Discipline (VIII, 1-19), (Isa. 40:3), (Matt. 3:3), (Jo. 1:23).

pertaining to the "preparing the way for the coming of the Lord."*

It has been described as a probability by several scholars, that during the revolt of the Jews, the masters at Qumran took up arms to defend their "holy of holies," whereupon the building was destroyed and its occupants put to the sword. However, this notion overlooks the most important evidence to the contrary.

Josephus tells us that these "holy ones" faced torture and death gladly rather than renounce or profane their beliefs, a principle of which was their non-violent way of life.

Philo also tells us that no maker of warlike weapons was to be found among them. They were called "Sons of Peace" because of their passive resistance to violence.

It is quite unlikely, therefore, that these devout souls took to the sword against the Romans.

Philo of Alexandria, who was probably the inventor of the word *Essenoi* which Josephus later referred to as *Essens*, appears to be the only truly contemporary source of our information about the sect. His *Quod Omnis Probus Liber* was written c. 20 A.D., or nearly a half century before the revolt of the Jews.

Pliny, the Elder, in his *Historica Naturalis* (ca. 70-77 A.D.) describes those whom he calls "Hessenes" as living a peaceful celibate, or priestly life, at a place not far from the Dead Sea. However, Pliny freely admits that he borrowed extensively from earlier sources. Even a casual reading of his essay tells us that he wrote historically and not contemporaneously about the sect, the same as did Porphyry, Dio Chrysostom, Hippolytus, Eusebius and other later writers.

And now as to the references of Josephus on the "Essenes": if he intended these to conform chronologically in time with other events and personalities among which they were placed, it appears that his first reference relates to about 160-142 B.C. and others to 6-8 A.D.

However, Josephus again refers to "our war with the Romans" (A.D. 68-70) in describing another event which he associates with those whom he calls Essenes. It is quite obvious here that Josephus was guilty of a confusion of identities. He writes: "They scorn the miseries of life and are above pain, by the generosity of their mind. And as for death, if it be for their glory they esteem it better than living always. Indeed, our war with the Romans gave abundant evidence what great souls they had in their trials, wherein they were tortured and distorted, burned and torn to pieces, and sent through all kinds of torture and torment, that they might blaspheme their legislator, or to eat what was forbidden of them,* yet could they not be made to do either of them, no, nor once to flatter their tormentors, or to shed a tear. Rather, they smiled in their pains, and laughed those to scorn who inflicted the torments upon them, and resigned up their souls with great willingness as expecting to receive them again." [16]

Here Josephus records a vividly true-to-form example of the attitudes of those who believed in the victory of Jesus Christ over death. Indeed, the word "Legislator" ** as used in this context is more applicable to the "Righteous Teacher" of the New Covenant than it is to the traditional Lawgiver of the Old Covenant. In fact, the entire narrative is clearly descriptive of early Christian martyrdom.

Josephus tells us that the Roman approach to Caesarea brought about panic among the people and they fled to the mountains. No doubt many of the inhabitants of the Jerusalem area likewise fled to isolated places.

---

* This eating of what was forbidden will be more clearly understood as the reader continues.

** Dupont-Sommer is also of the opinion that the Legislator referred to here is not Moses, because Josephus generally mentions Moses by name (*The Dead Sea Scrolls*, p. 91).

It is entirely probable that when Roman soldiers came upon the desert refuge at Qumran it was inhabited by a group of "Palestinian Christians" who had sought sanctuary therein.†

It was probably these refugees taken prisoner by the Romans at Qumran whom Josephus referred to by the name Essene. ‡

We know, because of the non-violent doctrine of their master, that the "Palestinian Christians" would not have taken up the sword to defend themselves. Again, according to all references to the contrary contained in the reports of Philo and Josephus, it is unlikely that those called "Essenes" would have opposed the Roman soldiers with violence either.

Who was it, then, who engaged the Romans? Indeed, the evidence found in the area reveals the effects of violent conflict.

During the revolt of the Jews, the warlike Zealots were active in considerable numbers in and around Masada and Engedi, not far to the south of Qumran. Here, then, are the ones who stormed the Roman outpost at Qumran, probably in retaliation for the atrocities done to those seeking refuge there. It was probably their capture of the monastery and the annihilation of its defenders which again was avenged by the fire and sword of a superior Roman force.

* * *

Let us now return to our theory which holds that the "holy ones," the priests of the "Sect of the Scrolls" had, of

---

†This explains the skeletons of women disinterred in the Qumran cemetery.

‡Other examples of confused identity may be recognized in a later chapter. One begins to wonder to what extent the word "Essene" has been misused as a means of identity.

39

their own free will and choice, departed from Qumran to join with the faithful at Jerusalem.

In Acts 6:7 we read: "The number of the disciples multiplied in Jerusalem greatly and a great company of the priests were obedient to the faith."

Who were the great company of priests? Certainly they were neither Sadducees nor Pharisees. According to Josephus, the only other sect in Judea were those he called Essenes. It was a great company of their priesthood that constituted the holy of holies in the desert, preparing there the way for the coming of the Lord.

The reference in Acts 6:7 conforms to c. A.D. 30-33, before the stoning of Stephen, or before the conversion of St. Paul, A.D. 34.

We find, therefore, that the only logical explanation of the report in Acts is that the great company of priests* referred to are the ones we now find preparing to depart for Jerusalem.

Accordingly, the time is about A.D. 30.

News had come from Jerusalem which claimed witness to the death and the resurrection of one of their own brethren—One who had sat with them, who had eaten with them and had prayed with them. Indeed, One who had, unbeknownst to them, understood the hidden meanings of their sacred scriptures.

All this had been duly acknowledged and verified by the High Priest of the Order, who, after carefully checking the several prophecies, found that they had, indeed, been fulfilled to the letter. With assurance such as this, no doubt the brethren were filled with joyous anticipation, for had they not been faithful to the bringing to pass of the Age of Fulfillment? And were they not those who had actually prepared the way, the "meek," the "poor," the pure in heart,

---

*Josephus (c. 63) apparently refers to these same priests (*Life,* Chap. 1,3).

the peacemakers, whom the master had particularly singled out to bless? Indeed, they were the "Elect"—the chosen ones who were to preach the coming of the "Kingdom of Heaven."

Indeed, questions like these, and answers thereto when discussed among the brethren, must have brought forth many joyous "hallelujahs" and fervent "amens."

And now, after the excitement of the day and a night devoted to prayer and thanksgiving had passed, we find the brethren busily preparing to evacuate their "Holy of Holies."

The young among them were assigned the manual tasks, while the Elders who had endured the long and patient trials in the wilderness set about to perform the most sacred of work. Divided into the order of twos they began to sort out and to arrange for the safekeeping of the scriptures wherein was concealed the mysteries and the "Holy Word." The mysteries which only the "Righteous Teacher" understood and acted upon. The Word which made straight the highway for His coming, and the Word that made straight the highway He later chose to take.

The careful sorting, the cataloging, the wrapping of the Scrolls in linen, the moisture-proofing with wax, the placing in specially made jars, the capping and sealing of these and the placing of them high up among the stony labyrinths of the mauve-toned cliffs we have previously described in detail.

However, there is something strange about the manner in which these priceless documents were wrapped and stored in sealed vessels, for apparently they were intended to survive the ravages of an extended period of time. One might say that the men who prepared them for safekeeping were not contemplating in terms of their own generation, but rather of time many centuries hence.

How can one account for this? Did these master minds, gifted as they were in viewing the future, foresee the

41

necessity of preserving the Scrolls? Yea! for nearly two thousand years? Or can the motive be explained in other ways?

From time immemorial, man has been inspired or otherwise prompted to conceal and to preserve certain objects of value or objects of record. Every great monument has its secret chamber or cornerstone into which such articles and papers are placed. These are carefully wrapped and sealed to insure their preservation in order that peoples of a far distant time and culture might again read the message contained therein. So, also, might the ancient records which the "Holy Ones" so carefully hid away in one of nature's own monuments, have been deposited with similar thoughts in mind.

On the other hand, one might, if so inclined, read into this suggestion a purposive act far more profound than a mere desire to commemorate a point in time.

Whatever the inspiration or the inclination might have been behind the preservation of these precious documents, the fact still remains that almost 2,000 years have elapsed since the "Holy Ones," in a simple prayerful ceremony, intrusted their safekeeping to the hands of their God.

CHAPTER ONE
References

[1,5,7] Philo of Alexandria. *Quod Omnis Probus Liber.*

[2] Twelve Patriarchs (Zeb. 11:1), *Lost Books of the Bible,* World Pub. Co., N.Y., Cleveland.

[3, 8, 10, 12] Gaster, Theodore H., *The Dead Sea Scriptures,* Doubleday and Co., Inc., N.Y.

[4] Milligan, Rev. George, D.D., *History of Christianity in the Light of Modern Knowledge,* Harcourt Brace, N.Y.

[6, 16] Josephus, *Wars of the Jews*—Book II, Chap. VIII, 10.

[9] Josephus, *Wars of the Jews*—Book I, Chap. III, 5

[9] Josephus, *Antiquities*—Book XVII, Chap. XIII, 3.

[9] Josephus, *Antiquities*—Book XIII, Chap. XI, 2.
[11] Josephus, *Antiquities*—Book XV, Chap. V.
[13, 14] *Harper's Bible Dictionary*—p. 704.
[15] *Encyclopedia Britannica*, 11th Ed., Vol. III, p. 891.

CHAPTER TWO

The Recovery of the Scrolls

It is now the year A.D. 1947. Many changes have taken place in the world since the day the Scrolls were hidden away for safekeeping 2,000 years ago.

Mountains have been lowered, forests have been leveled, rivers have changed their courses, and green fields have become desert lands.

So also with the affairs of men. Nation after nation has risen to power, only to be lowered like the mountains, or leveled like the forests. The streams of life have taken many courses—some through green fields and others drying up in the deserts. False Christs have appeared in every land. Vain scribes and lying priests have garbled the teachings of the humble prophet. Men have done to others what they would not want done to themselves, and the precious blood of the Prince of Peace has cried out from the battle-soaked earth. Glory increased with glory as murder increased with murder, and the blind led the blind.

But all of life's streams have not led to desert lands. Many have gone to make the fields more green.

Contrary to the lust for power, the warping of souls and the prostitution of spiritual needs, the eternal search for truth goes on. Prophets, philosophers, mystics and poets of every land, truth seekers, men who cry out as did the prophets of old for loving-kindness instead of the sacrifice of life, have added living water to earth's green fields.

Man may falter in his quest for truth, but he will never abandon his desire to know.

However, even after centuries of seeking, the human mind is still unable to pierce the veil obscuring the answer to the great mystery of life. Even the most profound mystic cannot describe the prime cause behind the operation of the universe in terms other than the unknowable. The most learned of the great scientists can at best produce only relative answers which are necessarily contingent upon the efficacy of various electro-magnetic space fields, forces of attraction, repulsion, and the potential energy of matter in motion. But these are merely the implements of phenomena, themselves subject to a prior cause or causes, sequences in a chain which extends back and beyond toward the inevitable unknowable.

The prime mover of Aristotelian philosophy and the Godhead of the several religions have so far provided only a partial answer. Through these hypotheses they describe how it all came about, but they cannot explain "why."

Yet, the religious man is invariably in accord with the notion which gives purpose to all things. To him God designs, creates, and gives order to the changing elements of time. He leads man on toward new and more enlightening discoveries, enabling the human spirit to unfold, to obtain an occasional glimpse of the light of truth and love which persistently strives to shine within the hearts of men.

Such a man has little difficulty contemplating a cause behind the almost perfect timing which accompanies the movement of planets, the emerging order of the seasons, the beauty of form, the glory of color, the symmetry of design and the creative tendencies in living things.

Certainly, if the religious man observes and accepts these phenomena as the effects of a prime cause, he cannot limit his thinking in this direction, but must conclude that this same power also works in mysterious ways among the affairs of men.

Somewhere in the world new discoveries are made daily through the genius of man in his quest for knowledge. Unfortunately, however, most of his searchings are directed in channels more resplendent of material worth than they are of moral responsibilities. Rarely does his research add much to his spiritual stature, for shameful as the case may be, he has with few exceptions little interest in this direction.

Notwithstanding, however, there have been occasions where individuals have, without knowledge or foresight, been instrumental in the discovery of a particularly meaningful bit of knowledge while searching for something remote to its nature.

It has been said of such unexpected discoveries, that it seemed almost as if some mysterious power was directing the searcher. A striking example of this sort of thing is contained in the story of the shepherd boy who made one of the most amazing archeological discoveries of our age while searching for a stray goat. Thus was brought to light an exciting collection of old documents written during the first century B.C. and which throw a new light upon the origin of Christianity.

Certainly we, especially those who profess to be Christians, can hardly consider the circumstances attending this discovery as merely coincidental, particularly in view of the fact that both the area approximating the find and the find itself pertains directly to the God he himself worships.

Invariably, what one person recognizes as purposive another describes as accidental.

Was it then by the rule of chance that these carefully concealed documents were preserved for twenty centuries, avoiding thereby the torrid reign of religious despotism and the destructive zeal of its inquisitors? Or was there some knowing power which purposely withheld their discovery, awaiting a time when men would be free to decipher and to discuss their contents?

Shameful as the facts seem to be, it has only been during this twentieth century that men have been free to read, write and to express an opinion which might be considered embarrassing to canon law and practice without involving the hazard of being burned at a stake for heresy.

Whether we do or do not recognize in the recovery of the Scrolls a mystical influence at work, one must admit that time has been particularly favorable to their being brought to light.

Again, in discussing the means and the method through which the recovery was made, the same questions arise.

Was it mere coincidence that a wandering shepherd boy in search of a stray goat happened to throw a stone through a narrow opening high up on the rocky side of a cliff? Was it merely by chance that the stone happened to strike a clay jar? Was the resulting clatter of broken pieces merely an incidental sound, or was it the equivalent of a voice calling out, "come hither, lad, and have a look."

Whatever the underlying cause may have been, providential or incidental, the sudden unexpected sound frightened the boy and he ran away, later to return with a companion to explore the cave. The stone jars they found inside contained a wealth of old manuscripts.

"But to what purpose," one might ask, "can the recovery of these documents be attributed? Surely their contents must contain a more profound significance than to merely stimulate scientific study." Indeed, in a broad sense, this is a plausible question, but one which only the texts of the Scrolls can answer.

The Brethren, who carefully prepared these documents so that they would withstand the rigors of time, suggested that they contained a hidden meaning. To hypothesize an interpretation of this meaning might add to the evidence of "purpose" in the recovery of the Scrolls from a providential as well as a generalized point of view: i.e., considering "purpose" first, as predetermining the event, and second, as subsequent to the event, whereby the event motivates the aims and intents of those concerned.

In either case, if an inner meaning could be found in the texts of these old documents (this being the writer's purpose), one might, at long last, have a look in upon the actual circumstances and conditions which brought about the advent of the Righteous Teacher called "The Christ."

CHAPTER THREE
The Incarnated Teacher

The recovery of the so-called "Dead Sea Scrolls" has caused much interest and excitement among scholars and lay persons all over the world. What has influenced the most discussion among the several translators and scientists of Bible history is the shadowy figure upon whom the writers of the Scrolls seemed to depend for guidance. Thus from the Damascus Document we read: "And God observed their works that they sought Him sincerely and *He raised up for them a 'teacher of righteousness' to lead them in the way of His heart.*

"*All who do not lift a hand against His righteous judgements and His true testimonies . . . who give ear to the voice of the 'Teacher of Righteousness'—they shall rejoice . . . and they shall prevail over all the sons of the world . . . and they shall see His salvation because they have taken refuge in His holy name.*"* (C. D. C.)[1]

But who was this "Teacher of Righteousness" spoken of in the Essene Scriptures? To find an answer to this question scholars have spent many weary hours delving into the available records of early Hebrew history with the expectation of discovering a prototype of the one mentioned in the Scrolls, thereby revealing the identity of the Teacher of Righteousness.

---

* It is interesting to note here how this text taken from the Scrolls reads much like a passage from the pens of New Testament authors.

According to Millar Burrows, some scholars have espoused what may be called multiple interpretations. That is to say, applying the title "Teacher of Righteousness" not to an office in general, but to several individual incumbents of the office. [2]

Others identify the Teacher of Righteousness with Onias III who, "According to II Maccabees, was murdered at the instigation of Menelaus in the sacred grove of Daphne on the outskirts of Antioch.

"But nothing indicates that he was in any special way a Teacher of Righteousness beyond the statement in II Maccabees." [3]

"A dual identification of the Teacher of Righteousness has been suggested . . . according to this theory, it was applied to Mattathias, the father of Judas Maccabees, and also to Judas himself. It is hard to see any connection between either Mattathias or Judas and the Teacher of Righteousness of the Habakkuk Commentary." [4]

It is said the Teacher of Righteousness may have been a member of the Hasidic movement of the Maccabean age.

It has also been suggested that Eleazar the Pharisee was the Teacher of Righteousness. He is also supposed to represent the person of Judah through references to the "House of Judah." Again, he is described as Judah the Essene, whose predictions of the future were so astonishingly accurate. And once more, the name Zadok the Pharisee is described as being one of the supposed identities of the mystical Teacher.

All of these supposed prototypes of the person given such a prominent place in Qumran literature, have been more ably discussed by other writers. Further comment in this direction would be a repetition of what already has been said.

"For twenty centuries people have been asking who was this humble and gentle prophet (writes Dupont-Sommer), this suffering, righteous individual whose death saved

50

multitudes. In truth, apart from Jesus, the Christian Messiah, only one is known in the whole of Jewish history, and this one has only been known a very short time: it is the pious Teacher who was martyred by Aristobulus II." [5]

While, according to Dupont-Sommer, Aristobulus II appears to fit the role of the man of lies and the wicked priest, the part played by the martyred teacher in this connection is rather hazy. Was he the pious Onias who was stoned in 65 B.C.? Millar Burrows points out that there is no evidence that Onias was an Essene or that there is reason to believe that he was in any sense a Messianic figure who might have been the Teacher of Righteousness.

Dupont-Sommer further states that "The Galilean Master, as He is presented to us in the New Testament, appears in many respects as an astonishing reincarnation of the Master of Justice (Teacher of Righteousness). Like the latter, He preached penitence, poverty, humility, love of one's neighbors, and chastity. Like him, He prescribed the observance of the Law of Moses, the whole Law, but the law finished and perfected, thanks to His own revelations. Like him, He was the Elect and the Messiah of God, the redeemer of the world. Like him, He was the object of the hostility of the priests, the party of the Sadducees. Like him, He was condemned and put to death. Like him, at the end of time, He will be the supreme judge. Like him, He founded a Church (a New Covenant) whose adherents fervently awaited His glorious return." [6]

Here one might add also, and in accord with Essene Scriptures, that like him, He was the son of the Lord's handmaid, and like him, His disciples, after eating of his bread, turned their backs upon him, lifted their heels against Him and denied Him up and down. Again like him, He was outraged because of his entry into the temple, and like him, He was hung upon a tree or a cross made out of a tree.

Such astounding uniqueness of personality and behavior, and such amazing paralleling of events has never before been heard of as describing two separate individuals. Indeed, to even suggest that the evidence is indicative of two separate and distinct personalities is nothing short of treason to the processes of rational thought.

As both the Essene Scriptures and the New Testament appear to have almost identical claims of ownership to the same Saviour of the world, the question now is, according to Dupont-Sommer, "to which of the two sects—the Jewish or the Christian—does the priority belong? Which of the two was able to influence the other?" The reply leaves no room for doubt. The Teacher of Righteousness died about 65-63 B.C., whereas Jesus died almost a century later. In every case (continues the distinguished scholar) where the resemblance compels, or invites us to think of a borrowing, this was on the part of Christianity." [7]

Here one finds suggested the age-old notion which has from time to time doubted the historicity of the gospel Jesus. Certainly the recovery of this almost exact prototype of the Son of Man among the literature of the Qumran Sect adds new and most convincing strength to the viewpoint that the gospel writers borrowed extensively from the Essene Scriptures, that they made the many references in the Qumran texts to do duty for the bringing to life of their own idea of a Saviour of the world.

What a devastating hypothesis, for it places the gospel Jesus completely in the category of supposition, or myth.

Certainly, to say the least, providing this hypothesis is not countered with a more realistic one to the contrary, Christianity can no longer hold to its cherished idea of the uniqueness of Jesus.

In the past, this idea has been able to resist all the many similarities and parallels through which various scholars have attempted to link the uniqueness of Jesus with the founders of the several pagan cults and mystery religions.

However, today Christian defense in this direction can no longer be sustained by the wide differences in time, space, nationality, culture and tongue of these various cults—to the habits and customs of the Galilean, for now the newly recovered Messiah of the Scrolls reduces the question to a strictly Palestinian affair. It, therefore, would seem quite unsound for one to attempt to argue away the significance of one of these unique characters in order to justify the traditional importance of the other.

But suppose we review a few of the passages taken from scriptures which grew up out of the Sect of the Scrolls.

We find in these "pre-manger" writings some of the criteria which prompted the eminent French scholar Dupont-Sommer to make his startling comparison.

Among the basic scriptures used by the Brotherhood were the Book of Enoch and The Testament of the Twelve Patriarchs. Ten manuscripts of the former were found in the Qumran caves, a fact which is not widely publicized. They were written in Aramaic, the mother tongue of Jesus and the Sect of the Scrolls. According to scholars, the book had its origin and growth during the first and late second centuries B.C., which also parallels the period allotted to the organization and development of the Sect and the writing of the Scrolls. In fact, there are those among the scholars who insist that the Book of Enoch is an original sectarian Scripture. The evidence certainly does support this conclusion for here, as in other writings of the Sect, we find texts such as the following:

"For the 'elect' there shall be light and grace and peace, and they shall inherit the earth." (viz. Matt. 5:5) And . . . the Righteous One (Teacher of Righteousness) shall appear before the eyes of the 'elect' who dwell on the earth." (a)

"This is the Son of Man who hath Righteousness, With whom dwelleth righteousness, And who revealeth all the treasures of that which is hidden. Because the Lord of Spirits hath chosen him.

"And at that hour that the Son of Man was named in the presence of the Lord of Spirits (compare Mark 1:10,11), He shall be a staff to the righteous whereupon to stay themselves and not to fall. And He shall be the light of the Gentiles and the hope of those who are troubled of heart. (viz. "Blessed are they that mourn.") And all who dwell on earth shall fall down and worship Him and will praise and bless and celebrate with song the Lord of Spirits. And He hath been chosen and hidden before Him, Before the creation of the world and forever more (viz. John 1). And the wisdom of the Lord of Spirits hath revealed Him to the holy and righteous, For in His name are they saved." (b) (viz. John 3:17).

As to *The Testaments of the Twelve Patriarchs*, these scriptures were composed a hundred years or more before the Christian era, perhaps near or during the time of the writing of the Zadokite document. They probably grew up, and along with the "New Covenant" movement, for indications are that several amendments were made about the year 63 B. C., or near the time of Pompey's conquest of Jerusalem.

Parts of these scriptures have long been supposed to be the work of Christian interpolators. However, texts have been found identifying the very passages which scholars previously had supposed to be of Christian origin.

"The real point of the whole discovery," (writes Dr. Francis Potter) is that the Enochan and other apocalyptic books were found in great profusion in the Qumran caves and can now be dated definitely before Christianity. Their alleged interpolations by Christians can hardly have been made in 100 B. C." [8]

"These Christological passages," (writes Dupont-Sommer) "taken as a whole, henceforth seem to be of the greatest worth, and to continue to reject them *a priori* as being of Christian origin would appear to be contrary to all sound method. It is now certain—and this is one of the most important revelations of the Dead Sea discoveries—that Judaism in the first century B. C. saw a whole theology of the suffering Messiah, of a Messiah who should be the redeemer of the world, developing around the person of the Master of Justice." [9]

Inclusive with the book of *Enoch*, *Jubilees*, and the *Apocalypse of Lamech*, "I am convinced," continues Dupont-Sommer, "that other writings, in particular *The Testament of the Twelve Patriarchs*, should be assigned to the sect of the New Covenant. *The Testament of the Twelve Patriarchs* is an abundant harvest of texts relative to the dead and glorified Anointed One—a whole mystery of salvation perfectly elaborated. There can be no doubt that this Anointed One was the Master of Justice who founded the New Covenant." [10]

Martin Larson in his monumental work *The Story of Christian Origins* writes: "What scholars believed could only refer to Jesus we now know to have been written about the Essene prophet." [11]

For example, consider the following texts:

"And I saw that from Judah was born a virgin wearing a linen garment:*

And from her was born a lamb. The Lamb of God, who taketh away the sins of the world, (compare John 1:29, 36) Who saveth all the Gentiles and Israel". (c)

----

*The Essenes wore white linen garments.

55

"And his star shall arise in heaven, as a King . . . and there shall be peace in all the earth" (d) (Compare Matt. 2:9, 10 and Luke 2:14).

"For the Lord shall raise up a priest from Judah as it were a king, God, and man. He shall save all the Gentiles and the race of Israel.

"For the Lord God shall appear on earth in the body of man. He shall sit and eat with men and save them." (e)

According to scholars, "this concept could not have been written by a Christian because the Apostolic Church never taught that Jesus was God . . . it was, however, established among the Essenes that the ultimate judge of mankind would be both," [12] i.e., both God and man.

According to Millar Burrows, The Teacher of Righteousness was a priest* who was believed by his disciples to be endowed with power to interpret the words of the prophets and the law. (Compare Matt. 5:17).

"Then shall the Lord raise up a new priest.* The heavens shall be opened and glory shall come upon him, sanctified with the Father's voice uttered over him. And the Spirit of understanding and sanctification (Holy Ghost) shall rest upon him in the water." (f)

This text clearly prophesies the Baptism of the new priest, the sanctified "Teacher," looked forward to by the Sect of the Scrolls.

Now by adding to this a phrase taken from the Odes of Solomon—"The dove fluttered over the Messiah"— we find the gospel narrative (Luke 3:21, 22) to be almost a complete prototype of scripture written prior to the event as it is described by New Testament writers.

---

* Clement I in his Epistle to the Corinthians also refers to Jesus Christ as "our High Priest."

No one knows the origin of the Odes of Solomon, but when one compares them with the translations of certain Qumran texts, a remarkable similarity of both theme and form is immediately discerned.

One might ask here, was the New Testament story of the Baptism borrowed from scriptures which were written and used by the "Sect of the Scrolls" prior to the advent of Jesus, or, did Jesus offer himself in Baptism as the acme of inner conviction, so that these same scriptures might be fulfilled?

Here is another text, the references of which may be found in a variety of forms and constructions throughout the New Testament:

"A king shall arise in Judea and shall establish a new priesthood after the fashion of the Gentiles. And in his priesthood the Gentiles shall be multiplied in knowledge upon the earth through the grace of the Lord.

"And in his priesthood shall sin come to an end, and the lawless cease to do evil. And he shall open the gates of Paradise and give to the saints to eat from the tree of life, and the spirit of holiness shall be upon them.

"But the wicked shall act godlessly against the saviour of the world so he shall not bear with Jerusalem because of their wickedness, but the veil of the temple shall be rent and ye shall be scattered among the Gentiles.

But our "Father Israel" shall be innocent from the transgressions of the chief priests who shall lay their hands upon the saviour of the world." (g)

In the following passage a voice speaks to the "Righteous teacher":

"The Most High hast heard thy prayer to separate thee from iniquity that thou shouldst become to Him a *son* and a *servant* and a *minister of His presence.* (g)

Again, one observes in the following texts a selection of ideas which later appeared in the works of the gospel writers.

"The Lord shall be in the midst of Jerusalem, living amongst men. And the Holy One of Israel shall reign over it in humility and in poverty. And he who believeth on Him shall reign amongst men in truth." (h)

"He coveteth not gold, (See Matt. 10:9) he longeth not after manifold dainties,* he delighteth not in varied apparel.** (See Matt. 6:28, 10:10).

He doth not desire to live a long life, but only waiteth for the will of God.***

The spirit of deceit has no power over him, for he looketh not on the beauty of women, lest he pollute his mind with corruption. (See Matt. 5:28) There is no envy in his thoughts, no malicious person maketh his soul to pine away. For he walketh in singleness of soul, and beholdeth all things in uprightness of heart." (i) (Parallel with I Peter 2:22, 23).

And again:

"The Most High shall send forth His salvation in the visitation of an only begotten prophet" (j) viz., 'the only begotten of the Father' (Jo. 1:14). "And He shall speak to God as to a father, and his priesthood shall be perfect with the Lord, and He shall arise for the

---

* Here the writer refers to Ps. 141:4.

** The Essenes wore only a single white garment.

*** Jesus, according to the doctrine of the "will of God," died at the early age of 30-33.

58

salvation of the world" (k) for he is true and long-suffering, meek and lowly, and teacheth by his *works**
the law of God." (l)

"And the compassion of the Lord shall come, as man working righteousness and working mercy unto all of them far and near." (m)

"In Him shall be fulfilled the prophecy of heaven concerning the Lamb of God, and Saviour of the world, and a sinless one shall die for ungodly men in the blood of the covenant (viz. blood of the Passover) for the salvation of the Gentiles and Israel. He shall enter into the temple and there shall the Lord be treated with outrage, and He shall be lifted up upon a tree" (n) (compare with 1 Peter 2:24).

"And the veil of the temple shall be rent (compare Matt. 27:15, Mark 15:38) and the spirit of God shall pass on to the Gentiles.

"And he shall ascend from Hades (Purgatory) and shall pass from earth into heaven." (o)

Here we have a veritable synopsis of Christian doctrine written many years before the New Testament and before the advent of Jesus, which recalls the statement of the Church historian, Eusebius (c. 295 A.D.), referring to the Essene Scriptures as "the Gospels and Epistles which were not yet written." [13]

The burning question renews itself with added emphasis. Did or did not the gospel writers lift bodily the whole Essenian interpretation and description of a Messianic Saviour and lay it down again along with a profusion of elaborations in order to recapture a showy figure and make him live and real?

---

* Note here, the precedent for *works* as later stressed in the Epistle of James.

59

It is quite obvious that a negative answer to this question must be as rational and as logical as is the evidence which supports the affirmative.

However, up to and concluding this portion of our thesis, it appears that an answer to the contrary must be supported solely upon theological grounds, even at the expense of what from a rational point of view appears to be quite obvious.

Here, then, it might be pointed out that all references to the saviour of the world as set forth in the Essene scriptures were written by those who had been particularly chosen by God to reveal his holy word—that actually as prophecies they foretold the advent of Jesus called the Christ, which does not in fact detract from Christian theology but, on the contrary, adds considerably to its stature.

However, there is one very important condition which is overlooked here. The fact remains, whereas the evidence reveals all of the prophetic writings in question to have been rendered by and to have grown up along with the Essene movement, that the Sect were themselves not only the authors of their own revelations but also the biographers of the mystical Teacher whose likeness has been embraced by the gospel writers.

Therefore, unless the whole and complete idea of the New Testament Saviour God, whose priority is held exclusively by the Sect of the Scrolls, can be inherited without equivocation by Christianity, the uniqueness of the gospel Jesus cannot possibly be sustained.

But suppose we leave the situation as it stands for the moment and again take up our search for the mystical Teacher of Righteousness.

"For all our labors," writes a leading American scholar, "he remains a shadowy figure. We do not know even his name. There is no hint of his identity in our older sources. The Essene commentaries hide him under his scriptural title, the Righteous Teacher." [14]

It is interesting to note here that wherein the Essene Scriptures the Teacher of Righteousness appears as a shadowy figure, that this same expression has been used many times in describing the historical Jesus.

According to J.L. Teicher, writing in *The Journal of Jewish Studies*, the Teacher of Righteousness was none other than Jesus of Nazareth, venerated as the anointed one by the Ebionites, a sect of Hebrew Christians of the first century.

Of all the various attempts to identify the mystical Teacher reverenced by the Sect of the Scrolls, this idea appears, with some reservations, to be the most promising.

However, while containing a wide margin of probability, Teicher's proposal has not found too much agreement among scholars. Ebionite authority of the Scrolls would supposedly date much of their origin within the Christian era, while on the other hand, archeological evidence in general places their authorship prior to the Christian era. However, and notwithstanding, there is, as we shall later illustrate, more depth to Teicher's argument than might be seen through the narrowed scope of strictly scientific procedures.

Professor William H. Brownlee has suggested that "the motif of the Suffering Servant (Isa. 53) is applied to the Messiah and to the eschatological prophet in the Qumran literature adumbrating (overshadowing) the identification of Jesus with the Servant of Isaiah." [15]

Indeed, one may clearly read, and as clearly interpret, the many verses of the Qumran Psalms as particularly referring to the one who was wounded and oppressed.

> "They thundered abuse of me; in their hearts they reviled me. My heart was sore distraught because of their obloquy, which they did heap upon me. It was a constant pain, a fretting wound in the body of Thy Servant." [16]

61

These few lines are descriptive of what is to be found throughout almost the entire scope of the Qumran Hymns. The Suffering Servant is therefore very much in evidence as is the Teacher of Righteousness, the Qumran Messiah and as we shall later see, the "Essene Christ."

The New Testament writer of Matthew (12:18) says that Isaiah prophesied Jesus in his vision of the Suffering Servant. But now our new evidence apparently identifies the Suffering Servant with the Qumran Messiah. Here again, if the question arises, "To whom does the priority of identity belong, the New Testament or the Essene scriptures?" one must indeed favor the Qumran Messiah. Accordingly, the only apparent means of sustaining Christian tradition in this case is through resolving what seems to be merely a conflict of identity. This is to say, whereas both Jesus and the Qumran Messiah are traditionally identified in a spiritual sense with the Suffering Servant of Isaiah, then, also in a spiritual sense, they must somehow share a common identity.

Suppose, therefore, we pursue what is so clearly manifested that it has been overlooked in the competitive efforts of scholars to identify the mystical teacher with some remote character of Hebrew antiquity.

The door has been left open to this approach by Dr. Theodore Gaster who, with a single stroke, countered all previous speculations concerning the pre-Christian identity of the Teacher of Righteousness. He wrote: "The religious brotherhood represented by the Sect of the Scrolls did not believe, as has been supposed, in a martyred Messianic 'Teacher of Righteousness' who reappeared posthumously to his disciples and whose Second Coming was awaited. The title 'Teacher of Righteousness' . . . designates an office, not a particular person. The passage of the texts on which the sensational theory has been based has been misunderstood. The Brotherhood indeed looked forward to the advent of a prophetic and priestly Teacher before the Final Era, but this was not the Second Coming of a martyred Christ." [17]

From this, one may gather that those whom God had chosen to be partners in His eternal covenant looked forward to the coming of one who had not as yet appeared in the flesh—one whose coming and whose purpose, character and destiny had been foretold to them.

According to this most opportune, as well as plausible conclusion, one may now look upon the subject in a new light. We can now interpret the scriptures of the Sect of the Scrolls as actually having been fulfilled through the advent of the "Essene Christ."*

But this does not, as yet, counter the evidence which, as was noted before, contests the integrity of the gospel writers. It does, however, preserve the uniqueness of Jesus on condition that the Christ of the Qumran scriptures and the Christ of the New Testament are considered not as separate individuals but as comprehensive characterizations of a single spiritual personality.

This condition should not be too difficult to abide by, for there is indeed evidence, much of which develops as we proceed with our study, which sustains the probability that Jesus had been a student at the Qumran monastery during his adolescence and early days of manhood.

Evidence will also be presented later to show that Jesus maintained a close contact with the brethren during the period of His ministry.

And now, but from a mystical point of view which should invoke the blessings of theology, we note that the Essene scriptures describe the brethren as the "Elect," the "Chosen Ones" whom God had appointed to make straight the highway in the desert for the coming of the Lord. Thus in accord with Isaiah (40:3) their scriptures read:

---

* See *The Essene Christ*, by this author.

63

"Thou hast acted for Thyself and for Thy glory and hast sent among mankind those to be schooled in Thy council, to the end that they may indeed prepare the way; make straight in the desert a highway for the Lord." [18]

The significance of this reference is that these holy ones being the caretakers of an important responsibility, were also keepers of the word, guardians of certain mystic writings held sacred by the Brotherhood. Here we again refer to Eusebius, the great historian of the early Church who appears to have had first hand knowledge of this, or remarkable insight, when he said: "The writings of ancient men who were the founders of the Sect referred to by Philo, may very well have been the Gospels and Epistles which were not yet written." [19]

Certainly, if the Christian believes that God bestowed special knowledge and responsibilities upon any man, or group of men, mentioned in his own cloistered collections of ancient writings, then to be honest and sincere in his judgment he cannot fail to recognize, with equal reverence, the will of this same God as it applies to those spoken of in the Dead Sea Scrolls.

In this same train of thought, how can the Christian doubt that certain among these "holy ones" were also inspired by, or directed "subconsciously" or otherwise by the "will of God," to prepare certain texts, to forewarn and forearm one who was to come in a choice he was to make?

"With whom took He counsel and who instructed him and taught him in the path of judgment and taught him knowledge and showed to him the way of understanding." (Is. 40:14).

In accord herewith, much of the Essene works are written as though it were intended that one might read himself into the texts—that is to say, in first person wherein the reader himself becomes the subject concerned.

While this appears to be merely a theological hypothesis upon which a reasonable explanation of the motivations leading to the ministry of Jesus might be founded, its psychological implications are equally impressive from a practical and logical point of view.

Considering first the theological hypothesis, we read in *The Testament of the Twelve Patriarchs* (an Essene Scripture) where Jebulum tells his children "not to grieve over his death because he will return again to be in the midst of his tribe."

Apparently the "Sect of the Scrolls" held the human spirit to be transcendental; where the scriptures prophesy of a prophet, he, in due time will appear either as a spirit incarnated or as one reincarnated.*

Such a belief necessarily holds that some men are born in the spirit of prophecy—that they, through, or during, certain conditions of time, circumstance, or mental stress, are brought to realize their particular endowment and act accordingly.

Again, from a psychological or scientific point of view, one might justly suppose that Jesus, being exceptionally influenced and motivated by the prophetic contents of the Essene scriptures, actually "imagined," or if you will, "realized" himself to be the incarnated spirit of the "One" who was to come.

This is, in a manner, affirmed by the New Testament wherein Jesus appears as determined to fulfill the scriptures—scriptures wherein we now recognize in a more complete sense to be those particularly revered by the "Sect of the Scrolls."

---

* This belief must have been held in common by the early Christians, for in John I:21 the Baptist is asked whether he is Elias returned, but he answers simply "No," as if the question were otherwise a responsible one. The writer of Matthew had similar ideas, for he had the disciples infer that the people thought Jesus to be Elias or another of the prophets returned.

"Thou hast brought me unto Thy Covenant. Words flow freely on my tongue as it were trained by thee." [20] (Scrolls) See Isaiah (40:14).

Note also how this same realization is similarly described in Luke 4:18: "The Spirit of the Lord is upon me . . . He has sent me to preach to the poor," . . .

What a tremendous challenge was involved in such a course of activity, and what an enduring reward was promised to "One" whose spiritual fortitude qualified His acceptance, for the Qumran Scriptures say:

"Until the consummation of the Age shall he be in the synagogues of the Gentiles, and among their rulers as a strain of music in the mouths of all, and he shall be inscribed in the holy books, both his works and his word, and he shall be a chosen one of God forever." (p) (See Mark 13:9).

In fact, the various realizations, motivations, and emotional stresses, which Jesus later endured along with the tremendous spiritual responsibilities which He accepted as His own, were clearly premeditated in texts such as these:

"Thou hast sheltered me, O God, in the face of all mankind and hidden Thy teachings within me, until it be shown unto me that the hour of Thy triumph is come, And Thou, O God of mercy, hast in Thy bounty given me place among those to whom Thou art pledged. *Thou hast chosen me and sent me* as a Father to them Thou holdest dear and as a nurse* unto them whom Thou hast made exemplars of men." [21]

In these lines the word "Father" might be interpreted, theologically, as an earthly prototype or Son of the Heavenly Father: i.e., "I and my Father are one." (Jo.10:30) Also,

---

* Moses also referred to himself as a nursing Father. (Num. 11:12)

the word "nurse" identifies one who comforts and quickens the life of a patient as described in the following texts:

> "Thou hast sent me as a banner in the vanguard of righteousness, a symbol of truth and understanding to all whose way is straight. By the words of my mouth Thou hast set men's life to rights and to them that repent I am a source of healing." [22] (Compare Mark 2:5, 17).

It is interesting to note how the phrase "Thou hast sent me," as it appears in the Essene texts, is repeatedly emphasized in the gospel of John.

As previously mentioned, many of these texts were written in first person, as if to emphasize a most direct and personal means of preparing "One" for his messianic destiny. Consider the following examples:

> "Through me hast thou illumined the faces of full many, And countless be the times Thou hast shown Thy power through me: for Thou hast made known to me *Thy deep mysterious things; hast shared Thy secret with me,* and so shown forth Thy power. And before the eyes of full many this wonder stands revealed: Thy glory shown forth and all living know of Thy power." [23]

Here the secret of the mysterious things are revealed only to "the One." In turn, Jesus said to his disciples "Only to you is it given to know the mysteries of the kingdom of Heaven." (Matt. 13:11).

Again, in Matthew, we find Jesus speaking to the multitudes on the mountain:

> "And he opened his mouth and taught them saying:
> Blessed are the poor in spirit . . .
> Blessed are they that mourn . . .
> Blessed are the meek, for they shall inherit the earth."
> (5:1-5).

In the Scrolls the same theme appears, similarly arranged, but spoken in first person, as by one who had "realized" himself to be the "incarnated Teacher."

"In the mouth of Thy servant* Thou didst open as it were a fount as a wellspring of truth. As a herald of Thy good tidings bringing cheer to the humble, compassion to the wounded in spirit and joy everlasting to those who mourn." [24]

But now, another text from the Essene Scriptures which appears quite prophetic in supporting the Christian doctrine of the Messianic hope:

"I am come to know Thou didst open the ear of one that He might hear Thy teachings and deliver Thy chosen people from the 'uncleanness' which surrounds them. And Thou didst send Thy light and Thy wisdom that he might announce Thy wondrous tidings, and reveal them to all who would hear. Thou didst encourage Him by Thy mighty strength that he might achieve renown, for Thy name, and triumph in glory. [25]

Note here that where the Messiah of the Old Covenant was to deliver the children of Israel from their oppressors, and to establish a political kingdom after David, the Messiah of the New Covenant was instead to deliver them from all "uncleanness." *The latter course as prophesied in the Dead Sea Scrolls was the course followed by Jesus.*

And here again is a text that clearly sets forth the doctrine of the virgin birth, the doctrine of salvation and the doctrine of the resurrection.

"Thou alone it is that hath created the righteous One: *Preparing Him from the womb* for the time of Thy good pleasure to heed Thy covenant and walk in Thy ways.

---

*"I am come among you as he that serveth" (Luke 22:27).

Thou hast lavished upon Him the abundance of Thy mercies, and opened *all of his soul to everlasting salvation. Thou hast raised His inner glory out of the flesh.*" [26]

Here God prepared *the righteous one* from the womb for the time of His good pleasure in accord with the Prophet Jeremiah who said: "He shall be called the Lord our Righteousness." (Jer. 23:5-6)

Several times in the Essene Scriptures "The One" refers to himself as the "son of God's handmaid." For example:

"Reject not Thy servant, the son of Thine handmaid, for by Thine own words have I called upon Thee." [27]

This same idea is inferred again in the following text. Here also the words "or ever" seem to describe a remote dimension in time, such as, "In the beginning was the Word, and the Word was God." (John 1:1) and then later "The Word became flesh (John 1:14).

"Or ever (or before)* my father begat me Thou didst know me. From the womb of my mother (Thine handmaid)* Thou didst shower me with grace, and from her breasts Thou didst sustain me, and from my youth up Thou hast enlightened me with understanding of Thy judgments, and caused me to delight in Thy Holy Spirit." [28]

One may clearly recognize in these several texts that the Christian idea of the virgin birth came out of the prophetic writings of those who made the "highway straight in the desert for the coming of the Lord." For if one parallels the words, "And the angel said to Mary, the power of the Highest shall overshadow thee, and there shall be born of thee the son of God" (Luke 1:35), both the son born of a virgin as described in Luke and the son of God's handmaid

---

* Parentheses by author.

as set forth in the Essene texts are one and the same. In fact, in Luke 1:38 Mary refers to herself as the "handmaid of the Lord."

The doctrine of the virgin birth is in consequence legitimately Christian of a "pre-manger" period rather than a reconstruction of ideas taken from the various mystery religions, as some writers have proposed.

Next, as was noted before, the Essene texts say: "Thou hast lavished upon him the abundance of Thy mercies and opened *all his soul to everlasting salvation.*" This is to declare that through the "One" upon whom the Father has lavished the fullness of his mercies may be found everlasting life, for as the texts further state: "Thou hast raised his inner glory out of the flesh," i.e., hast resurrected his soul out of the flesh, or, as according to St. Paul, has put off the corruptible and put on the incorruptible.

Again, the same blessings of "grace" are set forth in the following text:

> "Blessed art Thou, O my God who hast opened the heart of Thy servant, directed all his works in righteousness and vouchsafed unto the son of Thy handmaid the favor which Thou hast assured to all mortal 'elect.'" [29]

As this text reads, God, through "His Son," or through the Son of his handmaid (one and the same) assures all mortal "elect" (meaning those who 'believe') of salvation.

Another verse from the Scrolls refers to those who reviled Jesus (Matt.11:19).

> "Thou hast made me a reproach and a derision to them that live by deceit, but a symbol of truth and understanding to all whose way is straight. All them that challenge me, Thou makest to stand rebuked, distinguishing through me the right from the wrong." [30]

The following Scroll passage is similar to a verse in Luke:

70

"Little did they know that my steps were ordered by Thee, when they made me a mock and a reproach. Though Thou showest Thy power through me, they regard me not, but thrust me forth from my land." [31]

"And they thrust him out of the city." (Luke 4:29).

When Jesus himself assumed the role of the incarnated teacher, or better to say, when He "realized" himself to be the one whose spiritual fortitude and whose coming the scriptures of the Brotherhood so intimately describe and foretell, He conscientiously endeavored to abide by all the terms of his chosen mission. Only thereby could He feel secure in achieving the promised goal. This realization prompted the carrying out of a carefully planned course of action, much of which must necessarily remain obscure in process until the final climax had fully revealed and identified him as the incarnated Teacher. Accordingly, Jesus is reported as cautioning the people "that they should not make him known because that which is written must yet be accomplished in me," or by me. (Matt. 12:16, Luke 22:38).

Apparently Jesus was fearful that too much talk might occasion his enemies to obstruct his plans before they could be fully realized.*

This whole idea of fulfilling the scriptures is emphasized many times in the gospels. However, as we have seen before, many of these sayings do not allude to passages in our traditional scriptures but rather to texts such as the following:

"All that ate of my bread lifted their heels against me; all that shared of my table mouthed distortions about

---

* That Jesus fully expected to receive "The Father's" blessing after having completed his mission in accord with the prophecies is evidenced in his disappointment when he cried out from the cross, "My God, My God, why hast Thou forsaken me"?

71

me and they with whom I consorted turned their backs upon me and defamed (denied) me up and down." [32]

Here we see foretold the deserting of Jesus that night in the garden by those with whom He consorted, by those who but a short time before ate of his bread, by those who turned their backs upon Him and fled, and by those who, as did Peter, "denied him up and down."

John 13:18 reads: "He that eateth bread with me hath lifted up his heel against me." The only difference between the Essene text and the Johannine text is that the former has a plural, while the latter has a singular connotation.

It is to be noted also that the Essene texts do not specifically incriminate Judas which, contrary to traditional beliefs, may be nearer the truth.* (See footnote)

In view of our new knowledge wherein Jesus planned out his own ways and means of fulfilling the scriptures, it is quite apparent that the centuries-old condemnation of Judas as a "betrayer in fact," is due to a misunderstanding. Judas was undoubtedly a confidant of Jesus. The plan had been carefully rehearsed between them. No one was to know, not even the other disciples in whom Jesus, as the scriptures reveal, had little confidence. It was they who betrayed, or denied, him, not Judas.

The gospel of John, written some time after the Synoptists, attempted to correct this lamentable error, even as it did the synoptic fallacy which made Jesus to eat the Passover.

John clearly states that Jesus had personally chosen the one who would betray him (13:18), editing and interpolations to convey other meanings notwithstanding. The words "what Thou doest do quickly" are not spoken to rebuke, but rather to inform Judas of the need to make

---

* A detailed analysis of the role of Judas is found in *The Essene Christ* by this author (at present, out of print).

haste in order to complete his mission before the night had grown too late.

If the rendezvous in the garden was not planned out beforehand, why would Jesus and His disciples have left the shelter and warmth of the upstairs room to go forth late in the night to sleep on the ground, for, as the Gospel of John recalls, it was very cold that night?

The facts of the case are that Jesus, with knowledge beforehand, went forth to effect a prearranged meeting at a certain place where Judas was to appear with the Roman constabulary, and thereby assure His condemnation and crucifixion the next day.

There are entirely too many angles to this case to properly present it in this limited space. Suffice to observe, however, that one does not "choose" his own betrayer. The very act of choice involves preferential leanings, especially wherein the choosing pertains to a mission of unprecedented importance. Also, let us not overlook the fact that the utmost secrecy was necessary, even if Judas were to be branded openly as a scoundrel, for otherwise Jesus' enemies would say that He made himself to conform to the prophecies.

Our evidence shows that Jesus did of His own free will and choice arrange for the several events which in due time were to be climaxed by His crucifixion. This He himself confirmed when, according to Jo.13:18, He said:

"I know whom I have *chosen*, but that the scriptures may be fulfilled." Obviously, the scriptures here referred to were those of the Sect of the Scrolls which Jesus, through a carefully laid plan of action, was endeavoring to fulfill.

Again, the same night in Gethsemane, according to Mark (14:49, 50) He repeats once more "but that the scriptures must be fulfilled," which is followed by the words, "And they all forsook Him and fled," or in accord with the scriptures which Jesus was about fulfilling, "they with whom I consorted turned their backs upon me."

Later the same night, in accord with both Essene scriptures and Matthew (26:74), Peter indeed mouthed distortions about Jesus. "He began to curse and to swear, saying, 'I know not this man.'" Thus Peter defamed Jesus and thrice denied Him up and down. As to the others with whom the Lord consorted, who turned their backs upon Him and fled, one might assume that they likewise, when challenged, mouthed distortions about Him.

But here again, in complement with the subject matter, the question presents itself as to whether the author of Mark, from which the ensuing gospel writers "took their cue," had invented the idea of the arrest in the garden using the Qumran texts as a framework. Certainly the evidence here seems to be hardly less than incriminating.

Let us be reminded again of the illuminating alternative which seems to all but nullify doubts in this direction. But to question the logic of this alternative, one might ask: "If, as the case is presented, Jesus was in the act of fulfilling the scriptures, how was He to know whether His disciples would react in accord with the prophecies contained therein?"

This apparently is not a difficult question to answer. Jesus no doubt was, and had been, aware for some time of the particular emotional and psychological makeup of His followers. He could have quite effectually anticipated almost every thought and action of theirs. He no doubt knew exactly what their reaction would be to the fear of becoming involved, when He arranged for His surprise arrest and surrender to His enemies that night in the garden of Gethsemane.

The fulfilling of this particular portion of the prophecies was indeed carried out according to His prior knowledge of the character of His followers. He even reminded Peter, before being taken by His enemies, that he would deny Him thrice, even as the Dead Sea scriptures had foretold.

The idea that Jesus was inspired to make himself to conform to the bringing to pass of these prophecies is completely in accord with the Christian teaching of divinity, for if Jesus were "divine," then certainly His own plans and preparations toward the fulfillment of Scripture was in consequence "divinely authorized."

Thus, the evidence as presented both in the preceding pages and in those which are to follow indicates that the Son of Man actually fulfilled the mission of the Righteous Teacher prophesied in the Qumran scriptures.

Jesus was no doubt an extremely gifted one of the brethren—one whose extraordinary insight and will-to-love induced the awareness of a "oneness" with the whole of creation, and therefore a oneness with the "Father"—one who would suffer even as it was written to become himself the evidence of everlasting salvation.

Completely resigned to the responsibilities which a choice of this kind involved, He accepted His destiny as the one through whom the Kingdom of Heaven would come to pass.

"To God I commit my cause. It is His to perfect my way, His to make straight my heart." [33]

"Thou knowest the nature of Thy servant: how I have not relied upon the things of the world. On Thy mercies alone I depend to make the shoot to grow to bring Thy triumph to flower." [34]

The Baptism, where according to John, "The spirit descended from Heaven and abode upon Him," represents the full bloom of self-realization. Henceforth, Jesus is convinced of His responsibility as the "incarnated Teacher."

As the evidence of proof previously cited and which is to be expanded upon in the succeeding pages identifies the Sect of the Scrolls and the Palestinian Christians to have been one and the same, the course followed by Jesus as described herein is most convincing.

In the first place, this theory favors the historicity of Jesus as set forth in the gospels and second, it defends and maintains His uniqueness which otherwise, as the case now appears, would be entirely without foundation.

The most promising tone of this theory is that the hypothesis of the "realization" of Jesus applies with equal favor to the opinions of both the believer and the non-believer—to those who refer to Jesus as a prophet, or an inspired Teacher, and to those who believe on Him as their personal Saviour. To the former, however, the word "imagination" would be more convincing than the word "realization"—one favors opinion and the other, belief. The very fact that this whole idea seems to hold together both from a mystical and a rational point of view affords it the blessing of a comprehensive approach to the truth.

It might be pointed out here that the "realization hypothesis" is actually supported by Scripture. It was introduced in the Aramaic gospel of Matthew, used by the Palestinian Christians. Accordingly, at the Baptism the Holy Spirit descended upon Him and a voice from Heaven declared, "Thou art my beloved Son: this day have I begotten Thee." * [35]

Again, as was noted before, the Scriptures revered by the Brotherhood say: "From the heavens shall come upon Him sanctification; the Father's voice shall be uttered over Him and the Spirit of understanding shall rest upon Him in the water." (q) Thus realization triumphs through the Spirit of understanding.

The words "this day have I begotten Thee," describe the full bloom of an inner conviction: Jesus himself became the Spirit Incarnate of the "Righteous Teacher," long conceived by the prophets of the Dead Sea Scrolls.

---

* This same phrase is also quoted by Bishop Clement in his Epistle to the Corinthians (A.D. 95, 96) which verifies the later editing of the Four Gospels. Quite obviously the origin of the phrase came from Psalms 2:7.

Evidence that Jesus was so regarded by His followers is voluminous. Teicher writes: *"Moreh Zedey* is usually translated Teacher of Righteousness, Teacher of Truth or True Teacher—a teacher who is at the same time a prophet—indeed, the culmination of all the prophets, for, according to the Habakkuk Scroll, God revealed to the True Teacher all the mysteries of the words of the prophets. The True Teacher is, in fact, Jesus. He is addressed as such in Mark 12:14 (R.S.V.) 'Teacher, we know that Thou art true'."[36] Other similar references from the gospels are: "We know that Thou are a Teacher come from God." (Jo. 3:2)

"Teacher, we know that Thou art true and teachest the way of God truthfully." (Matt. 22:16, [R.S.V.]) "We know that Thou teachest rightly . . . the way of God truly" (Luke 20:21,) and again: "You call me Teacher and Lord . . . for so I am." (Matt. 13:13 [R.S.V.])

In an early century gospel called *The Circuits of Peter*, Jesus is addressed as "The Righteous One" and "The Teacher of Righteousness." [37]

Even the Prophet Jeremiah said: "He shall be called the Lord our righteousness," (23:6), which is but another one of the prophecies which Jesus as the incarnated Teacher fulfilled.

Another rather mystical proof of the identity of the Teacher of Righteousness appears in an astoundingly prophetic paragraph found in the Essene Scriptures. It describes, in part, where men of war who returned with the man of the lie are to be annihilated. This man of the lie could refer to a certain *sicarii* assassin or Zealot who fanned the fires of revolt (A.D. 68) which brought about a terrible massacre and the destruction of Jerusalem by the Romans (A.D. 70).

The prophetic verse further states that, "the wrath of God will be kindled against Israel about forty years after the death of the Teacher of Righteousness." [38]

Strangely enough, the destruction of the temple as also foretold by Jesus, did come to pass. Both the city and the temple were destroyed (Sept. 8 A.D. 70) by the Roman emperor Titus Flavius. This took place on or about forty years after the crucifixion of Jesus, or, forty years after the death of the Teacher of Righteousness.

In view of all the supporting data as presented in this chapter alone, one can hardly doubt the validity of the case wherein Jesus appears to have personified the "Spirit incarnate" of the Righteous Teacher, whose coming was prophesied by the writers of the Dead Sea Scrolls. Further proof of this is apparent in the attitudes of the sect called Nazarenes, Ebionites, or Palestine Christians, who accepted Jesus as the One upon whom the Spirit descended to fit him for his mission. Obviously, these Hebrew or Essene Christians must have been convinced of the uniqueness of Jesus, that he was "the One" prophesied in Essene scriptures. Certainly, they would not have believed in him if the priority of the entire "Christ story," as set forth herein, was held by another, as suggested by Dupont-Sommer.

CHAPTER THREE

References

[1, 2, 3, 4] Burrows, Millar, *The Dead Sea Scrolls*, Viking Press, N.Y.

[5, 6, 7, 9, 10] Dupont-Sommer, *The Dead Sea Scrolls*, translated from the French by Margaret Rowley, Basil Blackwell, Oxford.

[11, 12, 35, 37] Larson, Martin A., *The Story of Christian Origins*, Published by the author.

(a) (b) Charles, R. H., D.D. *The Book of Enoch*, MacMillan, N.Y.

(c) (d) (e) (f) (g) (h) (i) (j) (k) (l) (m) (n) (o) (p) (q) (r), *Testament of the Twelve Patriarchs*, World Publishing Co., N.Y., Cleveland

(c), Joseph

(e), Simeon

(f) (g) (k) (r) (d) (q), Levi

(h) (l), Dan

(i), Issachar

(m), Naphtali, (e) Simeon

(n) (j) (o) (p), Benjamin

[14, 15] Cross, Frank Moore, Jr., *The Ancient Library of Qumran*, Doubleday, N.Y.

[13, 19] *Encyclopedia Britannica*, 11th Ed., V. XXVI, p. 793.

[16, 17, 18, 20, 21, 22, 23, 24, 25, 26, 27, 28, 29, 30, 31, 32, 33, 34, 38] Gaster, Theodore H., *The Dead Sea Scriptures*, Doubleday, N.Y. (Note—with apologies to Dr. Gaster, the writer has in several places condensed the texts by omitting a few lines of the original for brevity's sake. None of the intended meanings have been altered in so doing. U.C.E.)

[8] Potter, Francis, *The Lost Years of Jesus*, Faucett Publications, Greewich, Conn.

[36] Teicher, J. L., "Journal of Jewish Studies," 1951

CHAPTER FOUR

John the Baptist and the Essenes

The theory of the relationship of the Sect of the Scrolls and John the Baptist has been considered for well on to 150 years. Much has been written on the subject, but until the recovery of the Dead Sea Scriptures the evidence has not been clear.

Today, however, scholars, after studying these manuscripts, are generally in agreement that John actually was a member of the Sect.

The gospels tell us that John the Baptist was brought up in the desert wilderness of Judea: "And the child grew and waxed strong and was in the deserts till the day of his shewing unto Israel." (Luke 1:80).

Can we imagine John wandering about from childhood in the forbidding wilderness of Judea, growing up and "waxing strong" in the same "foodless" area which Jesus later selected as a fitting place to endure forty days of fasting? Again, can we imagine him as growing up alone in the solitudes of a desert wilderness and then coming forth preaching a doctrine which, in a broad sense, is identical to that of the Sect of the Scrolls whose monastery was in the same wilderness where John is supposed to have lived? Where did he get his doctrine of repentance, his system of baptism and his vegetarian practices?

An answer to these questions must indeed be conclusive with the evidence which points directly to the Qumran monastery.

That John was, or had been, a member of the Sect of the Scrolls can hardly be doubted. Again, it can scarcely be doubted that his disciples were also of this same sect.

Professor Brownlee suggests that the "Essenes may have adopted John as a boy." [1] Josephus says, "they choose out other persons' children while they are pliable and fit for learning: and esteeme them to be of their kindred and form them according to their own manners." [2]

In accord with Isaiah 40:3, the brethren at Qumran were preparing the way, making straight the highway in the desert for the Lord. (1 QS VIII 12-14 D.S.D.)

Likewise, John the Baptist was devoted to preparing the way of the Lord in the wilderness. Like the Essenes, he insisted that without previous spiritual cleansing, bathing in water cannot remove guilt. Having succeeded in purifying his own soul through abstaining from all things adverse to God's commandments, as did the brethren at Qumran, he came forward to admonish and to encourage others to do likewise. "Repent," said he, "for the kingdom of God is at hand." Repentance was important to the "holy One's" doctrine.

According to Professor Fritsch, "John became convinced that the Essenes were not fulfilling (Is. 40:3) because they were preparing only themselves and not the nation as a whole for the coming of the Messiah, and so he left them and carried on a vigorous program of baptizing and preaching in the Jordan valley, in the belief that this did fulfill the prophecy of Isaiah and prepare the way for the Messiah." [3]

> "And by thee shall the Lord appear among men. Thou shalt stand near the Lord, and shalt be his minister and *shalt proclaim concerning him that shall redeem Israel*." [4]

In texts such as these, taken from scriptures found in the caves at Qumran, we find what might well have been the motivation prompting John to claim himself to be the voice of the one crying in the wilderness, or the one to "proclaim concerning him that shall redeem Israel."

> "So am I come to know that in Thy lovingkindness lies hope for them that repent and for them that abandon sin Thou bestowest freely Thy love. Therefore, though people roar, though kingdoms rage, I shall not be dismayed knowing that in a space Thou wilt grant Thine inheritance and all the forces of wickedness and all the sons of evil will be no more." [5] (Essene).

Thus we find John the Baptist on the banks of the River Jordan, about six miles from the Qumran monastery, the nearest habitation, crying: "Repent ye, for the kingdom of heaven is at hand." (Matt.3:2).

> "For he shall be great in the sight of the Lord, and shall drink neither wine nor strong drink and he shall be filled with the Holy Ghost even from his mother's womb." (Luke 1:15).

This reference in Luke has generally been interpreted to mean that Elizabeth dedicated her unborn son to the Nazarites. It is clear, however, that John did not take the Nazarite vows. It is known that the Nazarites abstained from any product of the vineyard, but it is also known that John abstained from eating the flesh of animals. This was not inclusive of the Nazarite vow.

The gospels say John's food was locusts and wild honey. (Mark 1:6). Some have interpreted this to mean the bean of the honey locust or the carob tree.

It appears, however, that the gospel report is in error due probably to a mistake in copying. A quotation from the Aramaic gospel of Matthew, (probably the first gospel written) and preserved by Epiphanus, describes the food of John the Baptist as "wild honey and cakes made with oil and honey." [6]

These cakes were probably made with corn, wheat or barley meal, a staple food of the Essenes. Here, again, if John lived in the desert, where else would he have obtained food of this kind but from the kitchens at Qumran?

"The Greek word for oil cake is 'enkris;' the Greek word for 'locust' is 'akris.'" [7] Thus it becomes quite clear how a mistake, intentional or otherwise, could have been made in the copying of the original Greek manuscript.

Now, all this is to verify that John had not taken the vow of a Nazarite.

However, as far as the report in Luke of the 'prenatal' dedication of John is concerned, this can now be explained as pertaining to the Sect of the Scrolls.

As was noted before, Josephus tells us that "they choose out other people's children and bring them up according to their own manners." [8] That is to say, they were brought up in the priesthood. No doubt it was the ambition of many a mother for her child to be chosen by the Holy Ones in the desert, there to be brought up as a minister of God.*

Evidences that prenatal dedications of this sort were considered holy unto God by the Sect are to be found in the Scrolls. For example, from the Book of Hymns:

> "Thou it is that hath created the righteous one, preparing him from the womb for the time of Thy good pleasure."

And again:

> "From the womb of my mother Thou didst shower me with grace." [9]

---

* The same can be said of James, the Lord's brother. See p. 91.

Thus, in accord with both the doctrines of the Holy Ones at Qumran and the report in Luke 1:15, John "shall be filled with the Holy Ghost even from his mother's womb." Thus was John dedicated by his mother to the Essene priesthood.

CHAPTER FOUR

References

[1] Burrows, Millar, *The Dead Sea Scrolls*. Viking Press, N.Y.

[3] Fritsch, Charles T., *The Qumran Community*. Macmillan Co., N.Y.

[2,8] Josephus. *Wars, Book II*, Chap. VIII, 2.

[4] Testament of the Twelve Patriarchs (Levi). *Lost Books of the Bible*, World Pub. Co., N.Y.

[5,9] Gaster, Theodore H., (Selected from the book of Hymns), *The Dead Sea Scriptures*, Doubleday & Co., N.Y.

[6,7] Goodspeed, Dr. Edgar, *History of Early Christian Literature*, University of Chicago Press.

CHAPTER FIVE

The Manual of Discipline
and the Epistle of James

One of the most trustworthy of New Testament writings is the General Epistle of James. It is commonly agreed that this document was written by James, the Lord's brother, who was an official of the primitive church in Jerusalem.

It is most enlightening to discover how closely this Epistle conforms to the doctrines of the Brotherhood. Indeed, one might place the writer as having been one of the priests* who went out from Qumran to reorganize the Sect in accord with the advent of the Essene Christ.

One may suppose that if this document were to be recovered in its original Aramaic, it might well be placed side by side with the Qumran literature, so closely does our present recension** conform to the Essenian thought. In fact, comparisons here might well furnish direct clues (Book of Acts notwithstanding) to the original doctrines of the Palestinian Christians.

---

* (See Acts 6:7). Also Josephus (*Life*, 3) refers to a certain company of priests who "being truly pious towards God supported themselves on figs and nuts", i.e., a vegetarian dietary, an Essene custom.

** Revising of a text.

In this direction, it is pertinent to note that the Epistle of James does not reveal any knowledge of the doctrine of "original sin" and the vicarious atonement as being the only means to the salvation of man.

Apparently James supports the Essene doctrine which rests the responsibility directly upon the shoulders of the individual as to whether or not he receives the crown of glory. That is to say, the Essenes held that every man is endowed at birth with the potential of knowing right from wrong. If he heeds the gift and seeks the light of righteousness, he will eventually achieve harmony with the great cosmic scheme. On the other hand, if he fails to heed the gift, and closes his eyes on the light of the true and the good, he will inevitably become lost in a morass of his own making.

All men are born not alone in the category of sin, but also in the category of truth and righteousness. Accordingly, man inherits something of each. He may, of his own free will and choice, either succumb to the spirit of evil or rise up to acclaim the glories of truth which are his eternal birthright.

This is a description in part of the Essene doctrine of the two spirits which God created to dwell in man.

It is interesting to note here how the Epistle of James refers to this same doctrine.

"Do ye think that the scriptures saith in vain, 'the spirit that dwelleth in us lusteth to envy'?" (4:5). The scriptures mentioned here are not our traditional texts, for nowhere therein can one find such a reference. However, we find the saying to be explained in the Scrolls—i.e., God appointed two spirits to dwell in us—the spirit of truth and the spirit of perversity. To this James says: "Draw nigh to God and purify your hearts, ye double minded." (4:8). In other words, of the two spirits, the spirit of truth draws you nigh to God.

The Scrolls say: "God created the spirits of light and darkness and made them the basis of every act, of every deed, and every thought." The one He loves to all eternity and the other He abhors to the end of time. But God will purify the heart of his creature, (his double minded) destroying the spirit of perversity from within his flesh to the end that being made upright, he will have acquired understanding of transcendental knowledge and the love of the "Sons of Heaven." In consequence, the evil spirit becomes jealous of the Spirit of Truth or, as described by James, "it lusteth to envy."

Some say that James wrote his epistle to dispute St. Paul's stressing of faith as the means of salvation. Others hold that the epistle was written even before the letters of St. Paul.

According to the latter viewpoint, the epistle must have been written some time before A.D. 45-70. This conforms to the probability that it was originally addressed to the communities of the Brotherhood scattered throughout Palestine.

Concerning the opposition of James to the emphasis put on "faith" by St. Paul, one can hardly overlook the fact that the Lord's own brother would be considerably more intimate with the Master's eschatological persuasions, than would have been one who never knew him in the flesh.

As to personal salvation, the Essene scriptures hold that it is "only through a spiritual apprehension of God's truth that man's ways can be properly directed; only by a spirit of uprightness and humility can his sin be atoned, only through the submission of his soul to all ordinances of God can his flesh be made clean; only thus can it be sanctified by waters of purification." (D.S.D.) [1]

Mere belief or faith in the existence of God will not save souls, for, says James, "The devils also believe and tremble." (2:19).

Contrary to the Pauline doctrine of salvation, James insists that only "the engrafted word can save your soul." (1:21). Only "the man who looks into the perfect law, the law of liberty and perseveres, being no hearer that forgets, but a doer that acts, shall be blessed." (1:25).

Here faith in the resurrection of Jesus is not the sure way to one's personal salvation, for this merely illustrates what one man can do. To Jesus, the word of God was the law and the same means to salvation was stressed by his brother James. "Be doers of the word and not hearers only, deceiving yourselves." (1:22).

"Let your good life be your works in the meekness of wisdom." (3:13).

"Wilt thou know, O vain man, that faith without works is dead?" (2:20). "For whosoever shall keep the whole law, and yet offend in one point, he is guilty of all." (2:10). Here James confirms the (Essene) doctrine which says: "They must not deviate by a single step from carrying out the orders of God." (D.S.D., 1,-15) [2] Or, as Jesus would say, "Not one jot nor one tittle shall be overlooked in the fulfilling of the law." (Matt. 5:18).

"Blessed is the man that endureth temptation: for when he is tried, he shall receive the crown of life, which the Lord hath promised to them that love him." (James 1:12).

We recall the many trials mentioned in the *Manual of Discipline* which, when undergone without temptation, lead to "Joy everlasting and a crown of glory." Again, James apparently speaks to the novices of the Sect: "Count it all joy, my brethren, when you meet various trials, for you know that the testing of your faith produces steadfastness." (1:2).

"Hath not God chosen those who are poor in the world to be rich in faith and heirs to the kingdom which he hath promised to those who love him?" (2:5). Here James refers directly to the holy ones at Qumran, to those known as "the meek," the "poor in the world;" i.e., "The congregation of the 'poor' who will inherit the Mount of Heights, The Elect of God's favor, Those whom He has chosen to receive their inheritance with the Sons of Heaven." [3]

Again, James says: "If any man thinks he is religious and does not bridle his tongue, this man's religion is in vain." (1:26). "Do not speak evil against one another, brethren." (4:11).

The Manual of Discipline particularly cautions against an unbridled tongue: "A man should not answer his neighbor defiantly, speak in anger against the priests, indulge in indecent talk, nor slander his brother," [4] i.e., his religious attitude is vain if he does these things.

"Is it not the rich who oppress you?" asks James. "Is it not they who drag you into court? Is it not they who blaspheme that honorable name by which you are called?" (2:6, 7).

The "Sect of the Scrolls" also detested the rich. "They accumulate not gold nor silver." (Philo) [3] "They eschew money." (Pliny) "These men are despisers of riches." (Josephus).

We note that James herein refers to "they who blaspheme that honorable name by which you are called." To what name does he refer? We know it was not "Christian" nor *Christianoi*, for this is a Greek name given to the followers of St. Paul. The Hebrew word for "Christ" is *Mashiah*, (anointed one).

The honorable name referred to could, then, be "Messianist." The Sect of the Scrolls were known as "Messianists," those who make the highway straight in the desert for the coming of the "Anointed One." The name also could have been "Nazarene," which has a similar meaning.

The Essene scriptures say, "Love each man his neighbor like himself." (C.D.C. VI, II-VII, 6a.) The same phrase is repeated by Jesus (22:39) and again by James (2:8)—"Love your neighbor as yourself."

"But above all, my brethren, do not swear, either by heaven or by earth or with any other oath, but let your yes be yes and your no be no, that you may not fall under condemnation." (Ja. 5:12).

Josephus writes of those he calls "Essenes": "Whatever they say is firmer than an oath, but swearing is avoided by them, and they esteem it worse than perjury, for they say that he who cannot be believed without swearing by God (by Heaven) is already condemned." [5]

Hegesippus (c. 160 A.D.) informs us that James wore white linen garments and eschewed the use of oil, two of the things Josephus says about the Essenes.

The members of the Sect "think that oil is a defilement and if anyone of them is anointed without his own approval it is wiped off." [6] Exceptions: if a bruised or sick person accepted it as a medicament, or as a healing lotion accompanied by prayer. (James 5:14). Oil otherwise used to scent the body was associated with the sophisticated social set. Its use in this manner was unbecoming to the simple man of God.

We learn from the church Father Eusebius quoting Hegesippus (c. 160 A.D.) that James, the Lord's brother, was holy from his mother's womb—drank no wine nor strong drink, nor ate the flesh of animals. [7]

Here we recall the case of John the Baptist, wherein the reports of Josephus and various references in the Scrolls, indicate that Luke 1:15 is better interpreted as conforming to Essene customs and practices.* The evidence that both the Baptist and James were vegetarian, and that both conformed otherwise to the ascetic practices of the Essenes,

---

* See John the Baptist, pp. 82-83

practices which were common to no other sect of people in Judea, leads to the conclusion that both were dedicated from the womb to those preparing the way in the desert for the coming of the Lord.

One might ask here: if Mary dedicated her later-born son James to the priesthood of the sect at Qumran, would she not have done the same for her son Jesus, later referred to as the "High Priest of God"?

Also, is it not clear that James' asceticism in meat and drink must be in direct conformity with the religion of Jesus, gospel reports to the contrary notwithstanding? A positive answer to these questions is apparently the only logical one.**

In closing this discussion on the relationship of the Epistle of James to the Qumran documents, it is the opinion of the writer that James was a member of the Qumran priesthood, and that "Primitive Christianity" was not merely an outgrowth of "Essenism" (a most misleading word), but rather a more intensified continuation of it.

CHAPTER FIVE

References

[1, 2, 3, 4] Gaster, Theodore H., *The Dead Sea Scriptures*, Doubleday, N.Y.

[5, 6] Josephus, *Wars*, Book II, Chap. VIII, 3, 5, 6.

[7] Bartlett, James Vernon, M.A., *The Apostolic Age*, Charles Scribner's, Sons, N.Y.

**Unfortunately, deletions and revisions were made in the Scriptures. (Editor)

CHAPTER SIX

A Search for Identity

Who actually were these people whom we have been referring to as Essenes? This is a question to which various writers over the centuries have produced only vague answers. However, through the light thrown on the subject by the recovery of the Scrolls, we are now able to view the picture with added perspective and dimension.

First, in order to make the best use of our new-found knowledge, it is necessary to examine the word "Essene." This task involves questions such as: How, and through whom did the word originate, and did the sect actually know of and use such a name among themselves?

To this author the first question calls for a bold answer and one that challenges proof of error: that is to say, the name "Essene" grew out of an invention of Philo of Alexandria who appears historically to be our prime source of knowledge about the Sect of the Scrolls.

Philo wrote about the "Sect of the Scrolls" as they existed some ten years or thereabouts before the advent of Jesus called the Christ.

Now as to the second question: the Sect used many expressions, as we shall see later, in referring to themselves, but to outsiders they were probably referred to as the Dedicated, the Pious, the Holy Ones, the Saints, etc. These expressions spoken in the dialect of the Sect, or in the Aramaic idiom appear as *hasyā*, or *hesē*, or again, *hasen* corresponding to the Hebrew *hasidim*—or pious. To a form of these Philo added the Greek termination—*enoi*; thus the word Essenoi. Later Pliny returned to the etymons *hasen* or *hese*, adding the Latin termination—*eni* and came up with the word Hesseni. Through the apparent anglicizing of these several constructions we now have the common name "Essene."

According to Professor Rudolf Bultmann,[1] the earliest church designated itself the Congregation of God. Likewise, the gathering whom Philo named Esseni designated itself the Community, or the Congregation of God. Bultmann writes also that the earliest church called itself "the chosen," "the elect" and "the Saints," all of which are names referring to the Sect of the Scrolls.

It is most enlightening to observe that the word "Saints" described both the earliest Christians and the Sect of the Scrolls. In fact, Philo said he used the word "Essenoi" to describe those called the Saints: "that saintly is the same word as Essenoi." (*Quod Omnis Probus Liber*).

The theory that Philo, being our prime source of information about the Sect of the Scrolls, invented the name "Essene" is supported by the fact that such a name is nowhere to be found in any pre-Christian Hebrew writings, nor does it appear in any of the Sect's own literature.

Here our search for identity resolves itself into the rather startling disclosure that "those to whom the name 'Essene' was given did not use that name in speaking of themselves. Nor was the name 'Christian' used by those who were the immediate followers of Jesus. The people who came to bear these names called themselves 'the Saints,' the 'brethren,' 'the elect,' 'they that believe,' 'they that are in Messiah,' 'they that are in the Lord,' 'the Sons of Light,' 'Sons of Peace,' 'the disciples,' 'the poor,' 'the meek,'" [2] etc. They were known as the Messianists, which word parallels the Greek or Christian. The names that applied to the Essenes are the same as those used by the Christianoi. Thus it might be said that the Sect of the Dead Sea Scrolls and their late First Century B.C. and pre-First Century A.D. brethren, better known as Palestine Christians, or Nazarenes (viz., Messianists) were in a broad sense one and the same people.

In other words, the Palestinian Christians were a party of the Nazarene Sect who had accepted Jesus as the "anointed One" and who had before his advent been called by Philo *Essenoi* and who were in turn the late First Century B.C. descendants of the Brotherhood described in and represented by the Dead Sea Scrolls.

But suppose we continue our search for identity through the throwing of a searchlight upon the origin of the Gospels.

"The tradition behind the Gospels was crystallized in Aramaic-speaking communities in Palestine and was not written down in Greek until the revolt of A.D. 66-70 against Rome had widely dispersed the Jewish Christians of Palestine and thus broken the chain of oral tradition which ties Jesus to the Apostolic circles." [3]

However, the first gospel was set down in Aramaic, not in Greek. It featured the mother tongue of Jesus and the brethren of the Scrolls. It was written in first person, Matthew being the one speaking in the singular and the Twelve Apostles speaking in the plural. It was used by the Essenian followers of Jesus who were also known as the Nazarenes, (viz. *Messianists*), the Ebionites, (viz. the *poor*)., i.e., the Palestinian or Hebrew Christians under the leadership of James, the Lord's brother. Thus it was referred to by Jerome, Epiphanius, and others as the "gospel of the Nazarenes," the "gospel of the Twelve," the "gospel of the Ebionites," the "gospel of the Hebrews," the last meaning the gospel used by the "Hebrew Christians" or those directly connected with the word as it came sweet and clean from the mouth of Jesus himself.

The Jewish Christians took special store of the saving elements in this gospel, necessary to the bringing about of the "Kingdom," as both Jesus and the prophet Isaiah (11:1-11) had foretold. "Herein is found the 'Essene Christ': he denounces sacrifice, the eating of flesh and the custom of slavery."

However, the humane practices of this little band of ascetics were completely alien to the prevailing customs of the Roman world. During these times the populations were made up of nearly as many slaves as free men and almost every household claimed at least one to serve the family comforts. No new religion, no matter how much it had to offer, could induce the heathens to renounce this family tradition.

Neither could, or would, such a religion succeed where the "doctrine of the flesh pots" held incontestable sway over the appetites of the people.

Now it came to pass that during these times several Jewish evangelists became fired with an ambition to convert the simple teachings of Jesus into a world religion.

Realizing the obstacles they must overcome to achieve this end, they preached into the new religion a doctrine through which both slave and master were made equal in Christ. They also interpreted abstinence from flesh-eating to mean those things sacrificed to idols.

Thereafter, and in accord with this doctrine, they produced a gospel given the name of Mark. It was written in Greek, as were the later ones which borrowed in part from it.

However, due probably to the absence of apostolic authority in the name of "Mark," another gospel was produced and accorded the name of Matthew. This gospel was intended to replace its original namesake. It followed quite closely in many respects the Aramaic texts, except wherein certain ascetic practices were stressed. These, as also in the case of Mark, Luke and John, were either omitted or were nullified through the use of various counter devices.

However, many of the same ideas, sayings, names and other characteristics common to both the Sect of the Scrolls and the Aramaic Matthew were written into the traditional books. This apparently explains how and why the New Testament acquired or contains so many characteristically "Essenian," or Nazarenian references.

But first, before we discuss these references, the name Nazarene needs some explanation.

In our New Testament recension of Matthew are the words: "He came to dwell in a city called Nazareth: that it might be fulfilled which was spoken of by the prophets, 'He shall be called a Nazarene.'" But the prophecy referred to is not to be found in the Old Testament; neither does a city by the name Nazareth appear here or in the Talmud. It is likewise nowhere to be found in the cartographies of the Maccabean period which extended up to about the year 63 B.C. It does appear on maps of Palestine under Herod the Great 40-4 B.C., but here the cartographers merely depend upon New Testament references for their information.

Josephus writes that the Roman Governor Varus sent an expedition into Galilee and took Sepphoris. He then pursued his march to the City of Samaria. [4] But Josephus makes no mention of a place called Nazareth, even though its present location is less than four miles from Sepphoris and had to be passed through on the way to Samaria.

Josephus is most thorough in describing the various towns of Galilee which were passed through or taken over by either his own armies or those of Rome. He even mentions many villages which either no longer exist or have been given other names, but nowhere, at least according to this author's research, does he mention a place called Nazareth.

Josephus also writes that he abode for some time in Cana [5] which, like Sepphoris, lies less than four miles from the place spoken of in the gospels as "Nazareth."

Much of Josephus' operations as an army commander were centered around Sepphoris, Mt. Tabor and the area where Nazareth is now located, yet he does not recognize such a place as existing.

Josephus wrote of events and places as they took place or existed throughout Galilee, a short time before the gospels were written. In view of these and other quite pertinent circumstances, one must conclude that the name "Nazarene" became a city called Nazareth through the writing of the gospels. (A.D. 70-125). Our evidence supplementing this theory refers merely to a settlement of ascetics who were obviously unimportant to the strategic accountings of Josephus.

But suppose we delve deeper into the subject continuing our search for identity.

In referring to the word "Nazarene," the most plausible derivation is found in the ordinary Oriental word *Nasara* [6] which means "Messianist," and again, as translated into Greek, it becomes *Christianoi*. The Hebrew words *Nazar*, (viz., dedicated) or Nazer, (viz. consecrated), also enter into its construction. To be consecrated is to be made holy, sacred, or saintly, which corresponds to the word (probably coined by Philo to suit his purposes) *"Essenoi."*

Thus, apparently from a resolution of the Hebrew *Nazar* or *Nazir* and the Oriental word *Nasara*, both having similar meanings emerged the name *Nazarene*(s): a sect whose community was later referred to in the gospels as "Nazareth."

However, in view of the fact that the several etymons refer and relate to the inner convictions of a people, rather than to a proper name, the priority of origin is immediately determined.

From these conclusions it is possible to reconstruct the origin of the place later called Nazareth. Apparently sometime approximating the year 40 B.C. a party of "Messianists," also known as "the Saints," "The Holy Ones," those dedicated to the law, or those consecrated to God, (viz. Esssaei) founded a community which became known as the place of the Nazar(s) (*Heb.*) or the "Nasaras," (Messianists), "Nazaras," and lastly Nazarenes.

One can now obtain a clearer understanding of how and why the author, or his interpolators, of the Greek recension of Matthew wrote "He came to dwell in a city called Nazareth," so that "he shall be called a Nazarene."

In view of our knowledge wherein the ethical idealism of the Nazarenes, so rivaled, spiritually, the doctrine preached to the Christians of the pagan world, the reference in Matthew has the earmarks of expediency. In other words, to confuse the fact that Jesus was indeed one of the sect of the Nazarenes, the gospel called Matthew establishes the Nazarene community in Galilee as "a city called Nazareth," even though such a city did not, according to our evidence, exist during the lifetime of Jesus.

Apparently, the prophetic note, added merely to strengthen the reference for its authority, has been questioned down through the centuries.

During the ninth century, the historian patriarch, Timotheus, wrote a letter to the Metropolitan of Elam regarding some ancient manuscripts which several Jews (A.D. 800) had found in a cave by the Dead Sea. He was particularly interested to find if the documents contained Old Testament texts which agreed with those quoted in the New Testament, and whether the prophecy "He shall be called a Nazarene" (Matt. 2:23) were in these manuscripts. [7] Here Timotheus also questioned the source of the prophecy whereby the gospel of Matthew claims its authority for saying: "He came to dwell in a city called Nazareth that it might be fulfilled which was spoken by the prophets, He shall be called a Nazarene." (Matt. 2:23).

We find (in Acts 24:5) that St. Paul was also identified as a Nazarene—not, however as a citizen of Nazareth, as suggested of Jesus (in Matt. 2:23) but as belonging to the SECT of the Nazarenes. This St. Paul does not deny.

We know that before his conversion, Paul was a member of the Sect of the Pharisees who were opposed to the Nazarenes. Therefore, one must concede, whereas St. Paul became a member of the Sect of the Nazarenes, that he did so to maintain himself as an example of the Nazarene Jesus.

CHAPTER SIX

References

[1]   Bultmann, Professor Rudolf, *Theology of the New Testament*—Charles Scribner's Sons, N.Y.

[2]   Davies, Rev. A. Powell, *The Dead Sea Scrolls*, Signet Key Book, N.Y.

[3]   Miller, Madeline and Lane, *Harper's Bible Dictionary*.

[4]   Josephus, *Antiquities*, Book XVII, Chap. X, a.

[5]   Josephus, *Life*, Chap. 1, 16.

[6]   *Encyclopedia Britannica*, 11th Ed. Vol. XIX, p. 319.

[7]   Rowley, H. H., *The Zadokite Fragments and the Dead Sea Scrolls*, p. 23, Macmillan Co., N.Y.

CHAPTER SEVEN

Other Verifications of Relationship

In a preceding chapter we discussed two alternatives: (1) Whether New Testament writers borrowed extensively from the scriptures used by the Sect of the Scrolls, thereby putting words in Jesus' mouth, or, (2) Whether Jesus had himself fulfilled these same scriptures, from which he quoted freely.

Our evidence seems to favor the latter alternative as being clearly supported by the several circumstances and conditions previously examined and as conforming remarkably well to the following testimonies which also bear out the identification of Jesus with the "Sect of the Scrolls."

That Jesus' sympathies were directed toward the brethren of the Scrolls is revealed, first, by the fact that he referred to them as true examples of the higher life in speeches such as the following:

"Blessed are the meek, for they shall inherit the earth. Blessed are the poor in spirit, for theirs is the kingdom of heaven. Blessed are the peacemakers, for they shall be called the children of God." (Matt. 5:3,5,9).

Now as to the *meek* who shall inherit the earth: "the Hebrew word for meek is *aniyim* and in the Aramaic dialect of the early Palestinian Christians the cognate term is used in the sense of *ascetic*" [1]; i.e., those who practiced abstinence. The Sect of the Scrolls were referred to as the meek or those who practiced abstinence. From their own scriptures we read: "All ye that are blameless of conduct hold fast to the (covenant) of the meek: the meek of the earth who (resist) all manner of (wrongdoing)." [2] The followers of Jesus became known as "the meek," for, as we shall see later, they also practiced abstinence.

Again, as to the "poor in spirit"—the "Sect of the Scrolls" were spoken of as "the poor in the world"—i.e., those who accept the time of affliction, but who will eventually be delivered from the snares of (death). [3] Here we see another mark of relationship between the "Sect of the Scrolls" and the followers of Jesus. The primitive Church called itself the "poor," a term which in the Psalms is associated with pious religion. The Psalms of Solomon, a scripture Dupont-Sommer assigns to the Essenes, [4] refers to the pious who constitute the true Israel as the 'poor.' "According to Origen C.Cels. 2:1 (1-126, 19) and Epiphanius 30,17,2 (1-3562), the Jewish Christians were likewise called "the poor," viz. Heb. *ebionim*, or *Ebionites*. [5]

When Jesus said "Blessed are the peacemakers," He most certainly referred to the "Sect of the Scrolls," for in His day they were the only people in Palestine who were qualified to receive such a blessing. They alone were known as "the Sons of Peace." They espoused a doctrine of non-violence which was unique among the Hebrews during the time of Jesus.

Again, Jesus addresses his sympathies to the Brotherhood. In the gospel of Luke he asks: "And will not God vindicate his elect who cry to him day and night? Will he delay long over them? I tell you he will vindicate them speedily."

According to the Manual of Discipline, the members of the community were the "elect of God's favor. They

101

keep awake a third of all the nights of the year, studying the Law and worshiping together" [6]; i.e. day and night, the elect cried out to God in prayer.

In *The Testament of the Twelve Patriarchs*, a sacred work which several leading scholars now claim to have grown up along with and out of the Essene tradition, appears a particular arrangement of words and phrases which substantially reappear in the Gospel of Matthew: (25:35,36).

> "I was beset with hunger and the Lord nourished me
> I was alone and God comforted me.
> I was sick and the Lord visited me.
> I was in prison and my God showed favor unto me." [7]

Now, the similarity of these texts with those of Matthew can be explained by one of two alternatives. Either the writer of Matthew purposely put his own version of these texts into Jesus' mouth, or, Jesus Himself quoted from memory a portion of scripture which He as one of the brethren had first-hand knowledge of.

The latter alternative being in accord with our evidence appears to be the most satisfying.

In reference to Old Testament prophecy and the doctrinal beliefs of the Essenes we find that, "to both the Qumran Messiah and to Jesus was applied the prophecy of Isaiah 11: "the shoot out of the stem of Jesse; and the 'Prophet' prophecy of Deuteronomy 18:18, are found in the Messianic testimonies document from Qumran as well as the New Testament." [8]

"The Lord has said unto me . . . I will raise them up a Prophet from among their brethren, like unto thee; and I will put my words in his mouth; and he shall speak unto them all that I shall command him." (Deut. 18:15,18), (Acts 3:22).

"Indeed, it is significant," writes Dr. Gaster, "that on a small fragment found in one of the caves that very passage heads a list of Scriptural quotations justifying the Messianic ideas of the community . . . " [9]

Now that we know that the Sect of the Scrolls considered these prophecies as referring first hand to the Qumran Messiah, we cannot question as to which scriptures—the Qumran or the New Testament—the priority belongs.

Indeed, the gospel writers apparently infer that those whom Jesus called to follow Him had been previously indoctrinated with these Messianic ideas. For example, in the several narratives wherein Jesus meets those who were to become his disciples, He usually is reported as saying, "Follow me," and they do so without hesitation or question. If we are to believe this is the case, then ordinary common sense tells us that these men must have been previously indoctrinated to anticipate the coming of the "Anointed One."

The Sect of the Scrolls (Essenes) were the only ones expecting this to come to pass, and at almost any moment. Being religiously schooled in the expectancy of such an event, any one of them might have been fearful not to obey the command of one whose manner and bearing was superior to that of the ordinary man.

It seems, therefore, that only an Essene, or one who was at least sympathetic to their doctrines, would have responded so eagerly to the call of Jesus. Surely anyone belonging to, or in sympathy with, either the sect of the Sadducees or the Pharisees would not have heeded His command. Neither would He have approached such as these in the first place.

Now follows a most convincing bit of evidence, borne witness to by the gospel writers themselves, which reveals the close contact maintained by Jesus during His ministry with the Brotherhood.

According to Josephus, there were communities of Essenes in all the cities and towns of Judea, and their doors were always open to deserving strangers. "They have no certain city, but many of them dwell in every city: and if any of their sect come from other places, what they have lies open for them just as if it were their own, and they go into such as they never knew before as if they had been ever so long acquainted with them when they travel to remote parts. Accordingly, there is in every city where they live, one appointed particularly to take care of strangers and provide garments and other necessities for them." [10]

Here Josephus points specifically to the certain house or houses referred to in Matthew and Luke.

The instructions given by Jesus in Matthew to "the twelve" were the same as those given to the seventy sent out in Luke.

In Matthew He instructs them to seek out the houses of the worthy and salute them. In Luke the raised hand of salute is accompanied by the words, "Peace be upon this house." Here He says, "If the 'Son of Peace' answers," and again according to Matthew, "You are among the worthy."

The salutation, "Peace be with you," or "Peace be upon this house" was an Essene manner of greeting. The Essenes were known as the "Sons of Peace." This name they acquired through their passive resistance to violence in any form, either to man or beast. According to Philo, "they prohibited their people from manufacturing any type of weapon, even the peaceful kind," [11] which probably means knives used for butchering. They were truly "Sons of Peace."

The seventy sent out were mere novices. They were not as familiar with Essenic customs as were "The Twelve," for, as some scholars suggest, quite a few of the twelve were former disciples of the Baptist, who, as the evidence indicates, was an Essene.

To the seventy, therefore, He added these words of instruction: "Eat such things as are set before you"—that is to say, don't complain if the food is meager. Here Jesus anticipated the probable results of a poor growing season whereby the table of "the worthy" might not be overburdened with the bounties of Providence, for the Brotherhood (the Essenes) abstained from eating the flesh of animals.

According to Matthew and Luke, Jesus charged His disciples: "Take nothing with you for your journey, neither money, bread, nor extra clothes, for there will be those in every city ye enter into, whom ye shall find worthy."

Accordingly, Josephus says of the Essenes: "They carry nothing at all with them when they travel to remote parts, for there is in every city where they live one appointed particularly to care for strangers and provide garments and other necessities for them." [12]

Here the evidence is so clear that even the doubting one must agree that the houses of "the worthy" spoken of by Jesus and those referred to by Josephus are indeed one and the same.

In support of the relationship of Jesus to the Sect of the Scrolls, it becomes quite clear that wherein Josephus uses the name Essenes, a word apparently invented by Philo, (see p. 92) he is referring to the same sect who were otherwise known as Nazarenes, of whom Jesus was a member.

Our evidence seems to indicate that the word "Nazarene" came into use during the late 1st Century B.C., as a means of identifying the "Pious Ones," (see A Search for Identity, p. 97), those who probably descended from the Hasidim of Maccabean times.

The same can be said of the name Essene which was also an adopted form used to identify the same sect in the Greek and Latin tongues. (see A Search for Identity, pp. 92-97).

Even today, scholars invent names such as "The Sect of the Scrolls," "The Qumran Covenanteers," "Sectarians," "Qumran Sect," "Cave Sect," "Damascus Covenanteers," etc., to identify these same people.

However, none of these with the exception of the name Nazarenes, were known to the people they referred to, and none which might even include the name Nazarenes were used in speaking of themselves or of one another.

Neither was the word "Christ" nor "Christian" used by the Nazarenes or the Palestinian followers of Jesus. The names (*Gr. Christos*), (*Heb. Mashiahh*) or "Anointed One" (Eng. Messiah) were introduced by the writers of the New Testament several generations after the passing of Jesus.

It was probably near the year 100 A.D. before the Greek termination (*anoi*) brought forth the name *Christianoi*—Eng., Christian. The word first appears in Acts 11:26 and again in Peter 4:16.

However, the use of the name in New Testament literature was probably due to a later interpolation, for indeed its co-form "Christianity" did not appear until the second century. [13]

It is interesting to note that when the name "Christian" became known to the Hebrew Messianic followers of Jesus, they construed it to relate to "apostates" or "heretics," names which were later given them by the Roman Church.

One of the most important of the parallels which reveal the oneness of identity between "those of the way" of the early Church and "those who chose the way" of the Sect of the Scrolls, are the particular eschatological beliefs which they held in common. Both believed that the last days were imminent, that the final generation was at hand and that a new age was about to be born. Both discovered fulfillment, in their time, of the prophecy. Both looked forward to the coming of a Messiah, a righteous teacher, a prophet or a high priest of God. Both believed that through His coming the scriptures would be fulfilled: that He would, *or did*, come as a man to walk among men and to teach them. Both believed that He would be, *or was*, hung upon a tree—that He would, *or did*, die because of the sins of ungodly men. Both believed that He would *or did*, arise and ascend to Heaven, and both believed that He would soon return to judge the world.

Indeed, the Sect of the Scrolls was devotedly preparing the way in the desert in accord with the Prophet Isaiah, during the very time that Jesus was contemplating the advent of His Messiahship.

"No less interesting, and perhaps more exciting than their other connections with the Essenes (writes Dr. Gaster) are the many parallels which these texts (D.S.D.) afford with the organization of the primitive Christian Church. The community calls itself by the same name (edah) as was used by the early Christians of Palestine to denote the Church. The same term is employed to designate its legislative assembly as was used by that community to denote the Council of the Church. There are twelve 'men of holiness' who act as general guides of the community—a remarkable correspondence with the Twelve Apostles. These men had three superiors, answering to the designation of John, Peter and James as the three pillars of the Church (Galatians 2:9). There is a regular system of *mebaggerim* or 'overseers'—an exact equivalent of the Greek *episkopoi* or 'bishops' (before they had acquired *sacerdotal* functions.)" [14]

"*The Manual of Discipline* and *The Zadokite Document* may be compared, in fact, with the *Didache*, the *Didascalia Apostolorum* and the *Apostolic Constitutions*—the primary documents relating to the organization of the primitive Church." [15]

"Such parallels as these cannot be set aside as merely coincidental. No two sets of people could have possibly existed together at the same time, in the same place, living the same way of life, practicing the same customs and holding the same religious beliefs, which differed not only from those of the surrounding population but from the whole world, without being actually the subjects of a common identity.

107

All efforts made by the Church of both past and present to becloud the case at hand merely reveal a prejudice which, for reasons more sensual than spiritual, is fearful of the truth.

CHAPTER SEVEN

References

[1, 2, 3, 6, 9, 14, 15] Gaster, Theodore H., *The Dead Sea Scriptures*, pp. 35, 49, 50, 259, 270, Doubleday & Co., Inc., N.Y.

[4] Dupont-Sommer, *The Dead Sea Scrolls*, p. 95, Tr. Margaret Rowley, Basil Blackwell, Oxford.

[5] Bultmann, Rudolf, *Theology of the New Testament*, p. 39, Charles Scribner's Sons, N.Y.

[7] Testament of Joseph 1:10, 14, *Lost Books of the Bible*, World Publishing Co., N.Y.

[8] Allegro, J. M. *The Dead Sea Scrolls*, pp. 151, 152, Penguin Books Ltd.

[10, 12] Josephus, *Wars*, Book II, VIII, 4.

[11] Philo of Alexandria, *Quod Omnis Probus Liber*.

[13] Miller, M.S. & J.L.—*Harpers Bible Dictionary*, p. 99, Harper & Brothers, N.Y.

CHAPTER EIGHT

About the Differences

A thoughtful reader, while reflecting upon the contents of the several books written about the Sect of the Scrolls, asks the question: "What difference does it make whether Jesus was, or was not, brought up as a member of the Essene sect, and why do some writers stress the evidence which indicates that he was one of the brethren, while others endeavor to show the same evidence to be misleading?"

A fair answer to the second part of this question is that on one side are those who never leave a stone unturned in their quest for truth, and on the other are those who claim truth to exist only in the writings of men of ancient times.

This is to say, one side concerns the attitude of the truth seeker—his thought and his endeavors, which in this case, are to recover a more complete picture of the historical Jesus, of his times, his character, his ethical teachings and his practices. On the other are those who claim that the new Testament alone contains the only complete and final word regarding the attitude of Jesus and his teachings, and that any and all thoughts, ideas, theories, or evidences of any kind which differ from, or tend to alter in any way the authority of the written word, are to be contested as false.

However, the facts are, as any well informed theologian will not hesitate to admit, that the New Testament does not report the complete story of Jesus and his teachings. Much has never been told and much has been inaccurately narrated or copied concerning his way of life.

For example, nowhere in the four Gospels, nor in the Epistles of St. Paul, is Jesus portrayed as *humane*. On the contrary, he is made a party to the betrayal of the very lamb which he is otherwise pictured as loving and protecting. This is not merely a sentimental observation but rather a reminder of how inconsistently the New Testament portrays an all-loving and compassionate Christ.*

Referring to the so-called differences in the sayings of Jesus and certain texts of the Scrolls, one cannot overlook the fact that the four Gospels were written largely through hearsay. They were written in Greek, alien to the mother tongue of Jesus, by men who never saw him nor heard him speak.

There is hardly a single scholar among Bible exegetists who will not agree that there are many inconsistencies and contradictions to be found in the Gospels and the Epistles. Many passages are known to vary distinctly from others describing the same events, many to differ from the original documents, and many which otherwise appear as suspect.

On the other hand, one finds in the Scriptures written and used by the Qumran sect many non-conforming and contradictory passages. *The Zadokite Document* clearly differs in doctrine from *The Manual of Discipline*. Even the latter document is found to contain many texts which are confusing in their intended meaning.

------

* A more extensive inquiry into the way of life of the historical Jesus is found in this author's book *The Essene Christ*. (Now out of print.)

Consequently, it seems rather presumptuous for one to pose a particular saying of the Gospel Jesus against a particular passage in the Scrolls in order to either prove or disprove his identify with the Qumran sect.

The Manual of Discipline states that one is to "bear hatred toward all men of ill repute, and to be minded to keep in seclusion from them."[1]

This passage has been selected to illustrate a difference between the attitude of Jesus and the writers of the Scrolls. It has been pointed out that Jesus said: "Love your enemies"—that he did not keep in seclusion from men of ill repute, but on the contrary, sat and ate with them, to heal them.

However, *The Manual of Discipline* states that every year, as long as Belial continues to hold sway, there shall be a review to make men aware of their status in the eternal society of God.

"The priests are first to be reviewed in due order, one after another, in respect to the state of their spirits. After them, the Levites shall be similarly reviewed, and in the third place all the laity (the regular order of precedence among the Jews; cp. *Mishnah Horayoth*, 111,8) [2] one after another in their thousands, hundreds, fifties, and tens."[3] (DSD).

However, one might very well suppose that this procedure was not confined solely to members of the sect, for as the texts further state: "The object is that every man in Israel may be made aware of his status in the community of God." [4] (DSD) In other words, made aware of the measure of his soul life in the eyes of God.

Thus, the texts infer that, when the spiritual worth of *every man in Israel* is determined, those who qualify for membership in the Brotherhood, "must pledge himself (themselves) to respect God and man." (DSD).

The texts also say: "Anyone who refuses to enter the (ideal) society of God . . . cannot be reckoned with the upright. . . .The resources of such a man are not to be introduced into the stock of the community."[5] (DSD).

These texts suggest that the yearly reviews were also, in a sense, yearly revivals. The object was to remind *every man in Israel* of his spiritual inheritance—to apprise him of the true Laws as they were engraved on the tablets of old, before they were perverted by the hands of scribes and the tongues of lying priests.

Thus, it might be said that the sect called Essenes, even as have all other religious sects, either sent out missionaries among the people, or did not move to restrict or restrain the setting forth of duly qualified Rabbis to teach the Law and the Prophets—to proclaim the acceptable year of the Lord, and to warn the "stiff-necked" that the Kingdom of Heaven is at hand.

We find John proselytizing and preaching the Essenes' doctrine of repentance by the river Jordan, and Jesus ministering to the thousands, hundreds, fifties, and tens, sitting and eating with those of ill repute, for they were inclusive of all in Israel, to be made aware of their status in the Kingdom of God.

The texts which say: "One is to bear unremitting hatred toward all men of ill repute, and to be reminded to keep in seclusion from them" (DSD) mean, according to other Essene texts, that one is to hate the evil spirit that has possessed man, rather than hate the man God has created, i.e., "God abhors this evil spirit and hates all its ways to the end of time."[6] (DSD) Therefore, "to be reminded to keep in seclusion from men of ill repute," (DSD) means "leave it to them to pursue wealth and mercenary gain,"[7] (DSD) i.e., to hate the evil, the uncleanliness which has engulfed them and to keep from being similarly corrupted. In other words, one is to consider evil as an abomination, as a thing to hate in itself, for the texts refer to "*what* one is to love and *what* one is to hate" (DSD), rather than *whom* one is to love or *whom* one is to hate."

112

This is apparently the way Jesus interpreted these same texts. He did not hate the Pharisees nor the Sadducees as people or persons, but he spoke out against the customs and practices which obscured their better nature.

Again, we read what appears to be a clarification of the passage on bearing hatred, for the texts further say: "One is not to bear hatred in the inner recesses of his heart toward his neighbor." [8] (DSD) Now as to what or whom one is to hate, it is indeed only in the inner recesses of the heart where love differentiates between the man and the evil which possesses him. Loving one's neighbor, in this sense, conforms to the teaching of Jesus on loving one's enemy. To love one's enemy "is not to bear hatred in the inner recesses of one's heart" for the man, but rather for the powers of evil, i.e., the political, the military, and the religious institutions wherein false Christs have possessed the bodies of men to do their bidding.

The texts say that when a person became a member of the Essene sect, "Everyone must pledge himself to respect God and man." [9] This does not refer to either the good or the evil in man, but simply to man as the creation of God. Philo, in his *Quod Omnis Probus Liber*, confirms this when he wrote: "their love of God, of virtue and of *man* passes all words."

One might say that the texts wherein one is not to hold hatred for his neighbor apply only to the relations of the sect among themselves and not to all men, which is contrary to the teachings of Jesus.

In view of the fact that this passage conforms to the one in Lev. 19:17 which refers to all the people and not to a particular sect within Judaism, one must assume that the Essenes, even as Jesus, interpreted it accordingly.

Considering the question of what or whom the brotherhood were instructed to love or to hate, we find that the texts of the scrolls oppose the idea that such as these are acquired due to the pleasures or the frustrations of daily living. The texts read: "all men are born and must walk in the two spirits that God has created in man: the spirit of light and the spirit of darkness. These are made the basis of every deed and the directors of every thought. God has appointed these two things to obtain in equal measure until the final age, at which time truth will emerge triumphant for the world. He will purge all the acts of man and refine for himself all the fabric of man destroying every spirit of perversity from within his flesh and cleanse him by the holy spirit from all wickedness." [10] (DSD).

"Men have walked both in wisdom and in folly. If a man casts his position with truth, he does righteously and hates perversity; if he casts it with perversity, he does wickedly and abominates truth. For God has appointed them in equal measure until the final age, until He makes all things new." [11] (DSD).

Thus, according to Essene Scriptures, every man, no matter what his trade, his business, profession or station in life, obtains in equal measure the spirit of light and the spirit of darkness. No man is totally evil, none without blemish, and no one all good. In fact, Jesus was in full agreement with Essene teachings when he said: "Why callest thou me good? None is good, save one, that is God." (Luke 18:19).

Accordingly, a brother in the sect could not hate his fellow man because of the measure which God had created in him, but he could be taught to love and develop the spirit of good within. ("The Kingdom of Heaven is Within"), and to overcome the spirit of perversity in preparation for the time when God makes all things new.

Thus, when Jesus sat and ate with sinners, winebibbers and gluttons, he taught in full accord with the Essene doctrine of the final age. He preached: "The Kingdom of God is at hand," that the time had come when God's Prophet was to cleanse men of all perversity.

In other words, and according to *The Manual of Discipline* we read:

"Until the coming of the Prophet . . . these men . . . shall judge by the original laws in which the members of the community were schooled from the beginning."[12] (DSD)

Obviously the words *Until the coming of the Prophet* say that when the Prophet cometh he shall make a new Covenant between God and his people. All rules, regulations, Sabbath laws etc., are to be reinterpreted and restated by the Prophet in accord with God's everlasting judgment, and he shall teach them the way to all truth.

Thus, it might be said that the sayings of Jesus, the Prophet or the Righteous Teacher, which may or may not have differed from the texts of the Scrolls, were later accepted by the sect called Essenes, Nazarenes or Palestinian Christians, one and the same, as the criteria of the New Covenant.

In the full sense of the word, Jesus was a reformer. As such he taught among his own sect as well as among those whom he referred to as the "Lost sheep of the House of Israel."

But even before the advent of Jesus, it is obvious that many changes were made in Essene doctrines and practices. The Essenes of *The Manual of Discipline* are considerably more advanced spiritually and morally than the Essenes of *The Zadokite Document*. The same could be said of the later Essenes of Philo, Josephus and Jesus. In contrast to the strict rules of the Zadokite scripture regarding the keeping of servants or slaves and the Sabbath ritual of animal sacrifice, *The Manual of Discipline*, while silent on the custom of slavery, is clearly against the ritual of animal sacrifice.

Writers on the Essenes who contend that the Sabbath rules of *The Zadokite Document* are contrary to the more liberal attitude of Jesus apparently overlook the fact that when Jesus opposed the custom of animal sacrifice in the

115

temple (Jo. 2:13-5) and again when he rebuked the Pharisees, (Mt. 12:7) he likewise opposed, as did the Essenes, the Sabbath sacrifice referred to in *The Zadokite Document*.

It was, therefore, quite in keeping with the attitude of the Essenes of his day for Jesus to expand upon his displeasure of the sacrifice and particularly the Sabbath sacrifice, by referring to other Sabbath rituals as "straining at a gnat and swallowing a camel."

Another one of the supposed differences between Jesus and the Essenes is the asceticism of the brethren, in contrast to the gospel reports concerning Jesus. In Matthew he is referred to as having "come eating and drinking," in contrast to the asceticism of John the Baptist.

However, a searching analysis of this gospel passage reveals a flaw in construction which alters completely the true meaning of the text.

In order to show proof that this passage is indeed in error we examine the case through the processes of inductive reasoning.

To begin with, it would indeed be contrary to all customary procedure or practice for the Master of any following to have exemplified a way of life completely out of step with that practiced by his disciples. Neither would such disciples have taught nor practiced a way of life completely out of step with that of their Master. Otherwise, and most certainly so, disciples would not be followers of a Master, nor a Master Lord over his disciples.

Therefore, in the case of Jesus and his disciples, if they, his disciples, had practiced a doctrine of abstinence, then it is clear that their practices are as witness to the teachings and the practices of Jesus himself. The historical truth of this statement will be discussed more fully in a later chapter, but to clarify our immediate discussion it is sufficient to note here that documentary evidence reveals the close associates of Jesus, the Apostles, John the Baptist, "James, the Lord's brother" and their followers, to have

116

opposed both winebibbing and gluttony, and to have abstained both from the drinking of wine and the eating of gross food such as the flesh of animals, two of the customs held in common by the Essenes.

Also, as discussed more fully in a later chapter, these same ascetic practices characterized the way of life of the so called "Palestinian Christians," the followers of St. Peter in Bythinia, and to a marked extent the early Christians among the Greek and Roman communities.

Now, posing this evidence as the criteria of proof in fact, suppose we again examine the passage in Matthew which reads as follows: "The Son of Man came eating and drinking, *and they say* behold a man gluttonous and a winebibber, but wisdom is justified by her children," or as the R.S.V. interprets it: "wisdom is justified by her deeds." (11:18, 19). Now what does this last line suggest? Clearly it points out that Jesus used the word "deeds" as pertaining to the slanderous tongues of his accusers, which accordingly represented the extent of their wisdom. In this case, Jesus does not admit of having "come eating and drinking," which is in accord with St. Paul who said: "The Kingdom of God is not meat and drink" (Rom. 14:17), but on the contrary, admonishes those who accuse him of such behavior.

All this is to verify that the phrase *"And they say"* as it now appears in Matthew should be returned to the beginning of the texts where, as our evidence seems to confirm, it appeared in the first century Greek manuscript, or in the original Aramaic Matthew. Thus, the passage should read; "And they say, the Son of Man came eating and drinking. Behold, a winebibber and a glutton. But wisdom is justified by her deeds." *Viz.,* The wisdom of such men is justified or measured by their deeds.

* * * * *

117

We return now to the beginning of this chapter, to the question, "What difference does it make whether or not Jesus was an Essene?"

The answer, first, is in whether those interested in the life of Jesus would or would not wish to recover a broader conception of who he was, what he taught, and what he means to the world.

Next, it is in whether the theologian would or would not venture to recover in Jesus the missing link connecting the common doctrines and way of life of the Essenes and primitive Christianity.

Again, it is in whether the custom of slavery which was accepted and practiced by Christianity for over eighteen centuries was or was not sanctioned by Jesus.

And lastly, it is in whether or not the doctrine of the winebibber and the fleshpots of Egypt are preferred over the humanely ethical countenance of the all-loving and merciful Christ.

These are but a few of the alternatives. However, even if the evidence were less conclusive in its support of the affirmative, one's choice may still be affected by traditional prejudices. On the other hand, it is to be hoped that wherein the higher moral and spiritual ideals of the historical Jesus are at stake, the seeker of the good life must justly favor his identity as the "Prophet of the Dead Sea Scrolls."

CHAPTER EIGHT

References

[1] to [12]—from translations by Dr. Theodore Gaster, *The Dead Sea Scriptures*, Doubleday and Company, Inc., Garden City, N.Y.

CHAPTER NINE

The Seven Proofs

At this time the author finds it necessary to repeat certain thoughts, scriptural texts, or other references previously discussed in order to clarify or strengthen the ensuing points of view. For this he asks the reader's indulgence.

In the preceding chapters we discussed the identity of a certain people—a people whom Pliny the Elder referred to as "a solitary sect, strange above all others in the entire world." In other words, a people whose customs, practices and ways of life were without parallel.

The Scrolls tell us that these same people whom Philo named "Esseni" existed for well over one hundred years before the advent of Jesus, the "Righteous Teacher," yet shortly after his crucifixion they seem almost to have vanished from the earth as far as the reporters of history are concerned.

Reason tells us that an organization, so long and so well established, numbering close to ten thousand people, would not have almost completely disappeared in such a short period of time. Certainly the war of the Jews with the Romans (A. D. 68-70) would not have resulted in their extinction, for many of the members of both the Sects of the Sadducees and the Pharisees survived even after taking up arms against Rome. On the other hand, our sect called Essenes, owing to their doctrine of non-violence, did not oppose the Roman armies, in which case their numbers would have been spared much of the results of the armed conflict. Also, and in their favor, besides being non-aggressive, they did not all dwell together in a single group, excepting, of course, the priesthood of the desert monastery, but lived as both Philo and Josephus tell us, in villages and cities throughout all Judea, a situation most favorable to their survival.

In view of all these circumstances and conditions, it is reasonable to hold that the Sect itself, in a large measure, continued to exist and to make historical record for some time after the death of the "Righteous Teacher of Galilee," whereas the name Essene did not, in fact, survive, historically, except through the prior writings of Philo and Josephus.

The early Church Fathers—Epiphanius, Heggesippus and Justin—have referred to several other Jewish sects, not mentioned by Josephus, who opposed the Pharisaic authorities and otherwise paralleled the Essenes in their ascetic practices.

However, evidence indicates that the sects referred to by the Fathers were not pre-Christian in origin. Names such as Dositheans and Boethusians (*Beth Essaioi*) refer to the Essenes. Their priesthood rejected marriage; all were vegetarians and believed in resurrection, in which case they were Christians and not pre-Christians. "The Sabaeans and the Masbuthaeans are difficult to identify and they have existed as such only in the minds of the Fathers," writes Professor Black.

According to Epiphanius, the Essenes were a Samaritan sect of pre-Christian times. There were, no doubt, Essene communities in Samaria who became known as the Samaritan brethren. Professor Black points to the probability that the Pre-Christian Essenic movement had its roots in the north. Indeed, our evidence points to Nazareth as an Essene community. Both Philo and Josephus report the Essenes as being widely represented throughout Judea, which actually means throughout Palestine. During the time that Philo and Josephus wrote about the sect, Palestine was the Roman Judaea which included Samaria and Galilee to the north.

Josephus also spoke of a fourth group in Judaism called Zealots—a party of anti-Roman patriots, which he distinguished from the purely religious sects—the Pharisees, Sadducees and Essenes.

The only other sect names of immediate interest are the Nazarenes and Ebionites. The word *Ebyonim* ('the poor') has become almost a proper name for the Sect of the Scrolls. The same term appears in Galatians and Romans as a name for the first Christians. Apparently the name Ebionite, which has been identified with the name Nazarene, or Nazorene, are one and the same with the name Essene. Epiphanius confirms this when he wrote: "Now the Nazorenes (*Nazarenes*) did not apply to themselves the name Christ or the name Jesus itself, but the name Nazorenes. And all Christians were at that time similarly called Nazorenes. But it happened that they were also called Essenes before the disciples began to be called Christians at Antioch."*

Thus, to be true to the basic factors of identity, we call to mind again that the Brotherhood was known and called by such names as "The Saints," "The Holy Ones," "The Messianists," "The Poor," "The Meek," "The Elect," "The Sons of Peace," "Those in, or of the Way," etc. And again we recall that these same names were also used to identify those whom tradition refers to as "Primitive Christians."

---

* See reference 10, Preface.

It now appears that when Josephus maintained that there were three sects in Judea—the Sadducees, the Pharisees and the Essenes—he must have considered the word "Essene" to be sufficient to describe a people whose beliefs, customs, practices and way of life were of one accord. As thorough as he was in his reporting, one finds it hard to believe that he would have omitted mentioning the Palestinian followers of Jesus.* Certainly if these people were, as we shall further illustrate, one and the same in nationality, in belief, in social, economic, ethical and religious practices, in fact in their total way of life, then it is clear how and why Philo and Josephus found the name "Essene" (*Holy Ones or Saints*) to be sufficient as a comprehensive means of identifying them.

It must be remembered also that the name "Christian" was not known during the time in which Philo formed his essay on the Sect, neither did Josephus use the name 'Christian'* in reference to the Hebrews, for this was a word completely alien to the followers of the Righteous Teacher and members of the first church of Jerusalem.

Accordingly, so-called "Palestinian Christianity" can be better understood historically as a continuation of, rather than an outgrowth of so-called "Essenism." The seven points which further illustrate this to be true are as set forth in the following premises:

(1)   That these devoutly religious people were the only ones in their part of the world whose common custom was evidenced by the wearing of a single white garment.

———————

* The reference to Christians in Josephus' *Antiquities*, Book XVIII, III, 3, has long been recognized by scholars as the work of a Christian hand. Even a casual reading of this paragraph reveals a style that is completely foreign to the hand of Josephus.

(2)   That they were the only sect in their part of the world who practiced an economy whereby everything was held in common.

(3)   That they were the only people in their part of the world whose religious leaders, or priesthood, practiced celibacy.

(4)   That they were the only sect in their part of the world who opposed the custom of slavery.

(5)   That they were the only religious sect, not alone in their own country but in the entire Roman world, who opposed the custom of animal sacrifice.

(6)   That they were the only people in Palestine or of the greater Roman world who opposed the slaughter of animals for food.

(7)   That they were the only people of Palestine and the outside Roman world whose way of life was opposed to war and the soldiers' calling.

We shall examine each of these seven premises, or proofs of relationship, first as it refers, or conforms to the custom and practices of the "Sect of the Scrolls," and again as it parallels the customs and practices of those whom tradition refers to as "Palestinian Christians."

(1)   Josephus tells us that the Essenes wore white garments as their custom. Some scholars attribute this mode of dress to Pythagorean or Orphic influence, as is to be noted in the following verse:

> "Robed in pure white I have born me clean,
>   from man's vile birth and coffined clay
> And exiled from my lips away touch of all flesh
>   where life has been." [1*]

---

* Confession in *The Cretians of Euripides* of one initiated into the mysteries of Orpheus. (See references).

Indeed, this reads almost as if it came out of the Scrolls themselves.

Similarly, the dress of the Essenes was white linen, worn as a single habit.

We see the followers of Jesus also wearing a single garment, that is to say, a garment of a singular material and color, or rather a cloth absent of color.

In *The Acts of Thomas,* a gospel used by several of the early Christian sects, Thomas wears a single garment in all weather and abstains from the eating of flesh, [1a] both of which were the Essene customs.

In the New Testament reports, Jesus reminds His followers to wear only a single garment when they seek out the homes of the worthy. (Matt. 10:10, 11). The gospel of Luke refers to those dwelling in the "houses of the worthy" as the "Sons of Peace," (10:6) a name answered to by the Essenes.

Apparently Jesus insisted that His disciples adhere to the customs of the Brotherhood, the Sons of Peace, in order to be accepted by the houses of the worthy. The wearing of a single garment without coat, purse or shoes, was a mark of identity which received immediate welcome into the houses of the worthy. (See pp. 104, 105 for further confirmation of this.)

Hegesippus, the second century Jewish historian, tells us that the custom of wearing a single garment was adhered to by James, the Lord's brother, who wore a linen garment only, as did the Essenes.

It has been customary down through the centuries to picture Jesus as wearing a white linen garment. This is said to denote purity, which was the same idea held by the Essenes. However, in order to complement color, which is an artist's prerogative, other dress materials are usually added but the single white material remains as a basic garment. Surely this tradition must hark back to some prior knowledge of a custom which was held as sacred by the

Essenes. No doubt, more extensive research in this direction would reveal other parallels between the Essenes and the early Christians regarding the custom of wearing apparel. However, this is a minor point of reference which is far overshadowed in importance by other evidences of proof which are to follow.

Now, as to point (2), everyone well read on this subject can recall how identically the Sect called "Essenes" and the "primitive Christians" held all their possessions in common.

The communal custom, as set forth in the Scrolls, is described by Philo as follows: "They had a storehouse, common expenditure, common raiments, common food eaten at common meals." [2] Again, according to Josephus, "For it is a law among them that those who come to them must let what they have be common to the whole order." [3]

In Acts 4:32-35 we read: "And the multitude of them that believed, (*those of the Sect*) were of one heart and of one soul; none said any of the things which he possessed was his own, but they had all things in common.

"Neither was there any among them that lacked, for as many as were possessors of lands or houses sold them, and brought the prices of the things that they sold, and distribution was made unto every man according as he had need."

In the Scrolls we read: "If there be found in the community a man who consciously lies in the matter of his wealth, he is to be regarded as outside the state of purity." [4]

We recall how in Acts 5 a man and his wife lied to the community in the matter of their wealth and were in consequence referred to, metaphorically, by the council as being among the dead as far as the community was concerned, or as the Scrolls say, "regarded as outside the state of purity."

125

It is quite evident that both Philo and Josephus, along with the writer or writers of Acts, are all referring to the same people—a people whom Pliny the Elder said were "strange above all others in the entire world."

The next item on our proof slate is point (3): the priestly practice of celibacy.

First, in discussing this point in relation to those called "Essenes," the several historical references regarding their community or communities are in need of clarification.

Josephus writes: "They have no certain city but many of them dwell in every city."[5] Philo writes: "At first they lived in villages and avoided the cities."[6] The inference here is that *later* they went to dwell, as Josephus reports, "in every city."

Pliny the Elder writes: "The 'Hessenes live on the west side of the shores of the Dead Sea. They live without women, renouncing all sexual love."[7]

Now it is quite obvious that Pliny is here referring to the inhabitants of the monastery at Qumran, and not to the Sect as a whole. The same can be said of Josephus when he wrote: "They neglect wedlock, but choose out other persons' children, when they are pliable, and form them according to their own manners." Again, he writes: "Moreover, there are other Essenes who agree with the way of living, the customs, the laws, etc., but differ in the point of marriage."[8] These quite obviously represent the family groups, the thousands who dwelt in every village and city of Judea. This is verified by the sect's rules for family life: "the relationships of husband to wife and of father to child." (CDC, vii, 6a-9).

It is clear, then, that the main congregation of the Sect dwelt in the various towns and cities of Judea, each group or community maintaining its own meeting place, or synagogue. Apparently, these synagogues were presided over by a teacher, or priest, who had received his instruction at the desert monastery. In other words, the building at Qumran was an *"Academe,"* supported by the Sect as a whole where those aspiring to the priesthood came to be instructed in the higher knowledge. Here, also, is apparently the place where, according to Josephus, children were taken in to be brought up as teachers or priests.

Now to return to the subject, it is quite clear that both Pliny and Josephus, as well as the Scrolls themselves, verify the monastic order at Qumran to be the abode of the Essene priesthood and that this priesthood was celibate.

Among the religious leaders of both the Sadducees and the Pharisees, marriage was customary. Priests and Levites married and passed on their offices to their sons. (See Lev. 21).

At the time of Jesus, the Essenes were the only Hebrew sect whose priesthood refrained from marriage.

Jesus has been referred to as the "High Priest of God" and as the "Righteous Teacher." James, the Lord's brother, was also spoken of in a similar manner. John the Baptist was called Rabbi, as was Jesus. All three taught the Prophets and the law as it was acclaimed by the priesthood of Qumran. And, again, all three refrained from marriage, conforming to the custom of the Essene priesthood.

St. Paul, following Jesus' example, also endorsed the custom of celibacy. In his Epistle to the Corinthians, he wrote: "It is good for a man not to touch a woman. I say, therefore, to the unmarried, it is good for them if they abide even as I." (1 Cor. 7:1, 8).

Down through the centuries various monastic orders have come into being. True to the example of Jesus and the precedent set by the Holy Ones at Qumran, they have maintained in a large measure the same ascetic way of life.

Celibacy among the priesthood of the present day Roman Catholic Church stands, apparently, on these premises and is but a carry-over, a continuation of a fundamental Essene or "Primitive Christian" custom.

We now discuss point (4): the custom of slavery. The Essenes were unalterably opposed to forced servitude. Philo writes: "Least of all were any slaves to be found among them, for they saw in slavery a violation of the law of nature which made all men free brethren, one of the other."[9]

Also, according to Josephus: ". . . .nor are they desirous to keep servants, thinking this tempts men to be unjust."[10]

On this Dupont-Sommer remarks: "How eloquently the ideas of liberty, equality, and fraternity are proclaimed in this religious society."[11]

Now what about Jesus: did he also oppose the custom of slavery?

This author writes, in *The Essene Christ*, as follows:

"We, as ordinary people, long ago recognized the injustice of slavery. In fact, many Christians have sacrificed their lives so that others might be free to choose their own way of life.

"If we, in our small understanding of justice and mercy, abhor slavery, did not He who fully understood these virtues still more oppose the system which robs men of their freedom? One feels that He was wont to weep for those so oppressed.

"Indeed, His concern *was* for the oppressed when He opened the book in the synagogue and from the sixty-first chapter of Isaiah read: 'The spirit of the Lord is upon me. He hath sent me to bind up the brokenhearted, to proclaim liberty to the captives.'

"Here Jesus, by proclaiming liberty, qualified himself as opposing any system or custom that captivates, binds, or in any way restricts the freedom of man."[12]

The same proclamation of liberty is clearly reiterated in the Epistle of James: "If you fulfill the royal law 'you shall love your neighbor as yourself,' but if you show partiality, you commit a sin, . . . So speak and so act as those who are to be judged under the law of liberty." (2:8, 9, 12).

When Jesus said: "Whatsoever ye would that men should do to you, do ye even so to them," He, in effect, challenged the slave owner to extend freedom to others if he would himself be free.

The Nazarenes, also called Ebionites ("the poor"), or the sect who represented the first congregation at Jerusalem under James, the Lord's brother, abided by the strict ascetic rules of their Qumran brethren. They held it to be contrary to the plan of God and the will of man for anyone to suffer his brother the throes of bondage.

However, at this point we find a parting of the ways, so to speak: Palestinian Christianity was to be taken over and amended by the evangelists who labored among the Gentiles. Materialism succeeded asceticism and human freedom became the first great ethic of Jesus Christ to bow to the carnal customs of the heathen candidates.

"St. Paul at this time was, no doubt, under great stress and pain in both body and spirit, for in assuming the responsibility of accepting the Roman custom of slavery, he was in consequence severely criticized and shunned by the old apostles. For this, and not the trivial disagreement on circumcision, was he called an 'Apostate.'" [13]

"The Greek democracies had slavery; the great landed estates of the Roman Empire were worked by slaves. The lot of slaves was often unhappy, and public opinion condoned the use of the lash on them, the killing of them when their usefulness was past, and the selling of them at a low price when they became old." [14]

"But St. Paul's sympathy was with the slaves. It was his hope that their owners' hearts would become softened upon receiving knowledge of Jesus Christ. No doubt many of the converts did free their slaves through becoming aware of the teachings of Jesus, but the greater part of them, while growing more sympathetic, retained their ownership.

"In an unprejudiced recognition of the spiritual and moral integrity of St. Paul, one must admit that any inferences favoring slavery in the epistles attributed to him, are the work of later hands, and do not represent the viewpoint of the great Apostle.

"St. Paul's letter asking forgiveness from a brother Christian for a runaway slave whom he is returning, is evidence that he did not approve of the custom of slavery, even though he did not oppose it as being absolutely taboo to Christian conversion. In his letter to Philemon, he expresses hope and faith that the 'Christ presence' would eventually bring about a reconciliation in the heart and soul of the slave owner.

"'I thank God always when I remember you in my prayers, because I hear of your love and of the faith which you have toward my Lord Jesus, and I pray that the sharing of your faith may promote the knowledge of all the good that is ours in Christ. Accordingly, though, I am bold enough in Christ to command you to do what is required, yet for love's sake I prefer to appeal to you as an ambassador for Jesus Christ . . . He (the slave) was parted from you for awhile, that you might have him back, no longer as a slave, but as a beloved brother, especially to me but even more to you in the faith and in the Lord.'" (Phil. 4-15).

In representing himself as the ambassador of Christ, Paul in this letter to Philemon, made it clear that the Master himself was sent to "proclaim release to the captives and to set at liberty those who are oppressed." (Luke 4:18, R.S.V.) The word "oppressed" in the King James translation is "bruised." A slave is both oppressed by his master and bruised by his lash. The suffering servant of Isa. 53:7 is similarly oppressed and afflicted (or bruised). Jesus read in the synagogue from Isaiah where it was further written, "And open the prisons to those who are bound." Past attempts to interpret these sayings other than referring directly to slavery have been merely to compromise the centuries-old guilt of the Christian community.

"During the 1840's, the Protestant churches of Virginia, South Carolina, and other southern states, actually passed resolutions in favor of the slave traffic,* notwithstanding the fiendish cruelties, inhuman tortures, suicides, and vile immoralities it embraced. It is doubtful if St. Paul would ever have used the psychology of "converting first and cleansing later" if he could have foreseen the future attitudes of his followers. But this was Paul's cross to bear. What must have been his inward struggle in discriminating between the ethical and the expedient! On one hand he was condemned for compromising the doctrine of Jesus and on the other he realized that in order to perpetuate in time the knowledge of Jesus Christ throughout the world, he must necessarily approach the heathen people through mitigation rather than condemnation. Thus one might recognize in St. Paul "the hand of Providence," keeping the flame alive in the hearts of men until a time when humanity would itself remove the compromise suffered by his inspired wisdom, and rediscover the New Covenant of Jesus Christ as it was known to him and the other Twelve Apostles." [15]

In summing up, we find that the stand of the Christian Church today on the custom of slavery is indeed the result of an evolved spiritual awareness—an awareness resolved in the Christian's heart through the mercy-loving spirit of Jesus Christ.

Thus, at long last, "the truth will out," as the saying goes, and again a common ground of relationship that was Jesus and the Essenes is brought to witness.

We now refer to point (5), the practice of animal sacrifice.

Even though our evidence concerning the opposition of the Essenes to this custom is overwhelming, there still exist a few items to be cleared up in order to be conclusive.

---

* Chambers Tracts, *Slavery in America*—publ. 1845.

It has been pointed out that a meticulous burial of animal bones had been found during excavation of Qumran. This, no doubt, dates back to an earlier period of the Essene movement. *The Zadokite Document*, a considerably older writing than *The Manual of Discipline*, provides for a partial observance of the custom of animal sacrifice, but later writings obviously oppose the custom.

In almost any of our own libraries can be found books which refer to slavery as an American custom, * yet this is not part of American culture today.

In many of our old New England churchyards moulder the bones of Christians who, by authority of their religion, burned women at the stake for witchcraft, yet Christians today shudder at the thought of their ancestors doing such things.

But this early custom of animal sacrifice by the "Sons of Zadok," was, as the later *Manual of Discipline* and the *Hymns of the Initiates* verify, replaced by more dignified overtures to God.

It must be remembered, also, that Qumran was inhabited almost 200 years, during which time several reformations must have taken place. Thus, the Essenes of *The Manual of Discipline*, the Hymns and the writings of Philo and Josephus, are more correctly of a time converging upon the Christian era. They were therefore considerably more advanced spiritually than the Essenes of *The Zadokite Document*.

On this point Dr. A. Powell Davies remarks: "The fact of change within the Essenic party may well be significant for the rise of Christianity." [16]

"One must remember," writes Dr. Gaster, "that Philo and Josephus are describing conditions as they obtained in the First Century, whereas our documents (the Scrolls) may reflect an earlier state of affairs and may even ascend to the Hasidim, Pious Ones, of Maccabean times." [17]

---

* For example, Chambers Tracts (1847).

Josephus writes: "And when they send what they have dedicated to God into the temple, they do not offer sacrifices, because they have more pure lustrations* of their own, on which account they are excluded from the common court of the temple, but offer their sacrifices themselves." [18] This report of Josephus has been subject to some misunderstanding. First Josephus says: "They send what they have dedicated to God into the temple." Certainly this could only have been a cereal offering, or more likely, a silver contribution, for Philo clearly states that they do not sacrifice animals. But in view of the statement that they were excluded from the common court of the temple, one wonders why they were otherwise permitted to send in an offering of any kind. Could it be that Josephus wrote down the word "temple" when he actually meant to write "synagogue?" The Essenes had their own synagogues in various town and cities of Judea. It was probably to these places that they sent, or rather dedicated themselves as an offering to God.

Josephus says first: "They do not offer sacrifices because they have more pure lustrations of their own" while again the texts read: "but offer sacrifices themselves." Certainly a "purer lustration" cannot refer to animal sacrifice, for Josephus has already stressed that "they do not offer sacrifices," meaning quite obviously the customary burnt offering.

However, when one studies the phrase "but offer their sacrifices themselves," it is quite clear that what Josephus meant to convey was that they *offer themselves as the sacrifice*, or, as Dr. Gaster explains it, "offered sacrifices within themselves." [19] Again, according to Dr. Brownlee: "They consecrate themselves to God as free will offerings," [20] viz., the giving of one's self in penitent restitution. Thus, in

---

* lustration:

A purificatory ceremony, performed as a preliminary to entering a holy place.

effect the human will sacrifices its carnal nature and receives the blessings of the Most High.

"The Torah—that is, the divine teachings (or guidance) as revealed to Moses—had, it was held (according to the Scrolls) been successively garbled and perverted by "false expositors. The communities' purpose was to exemplify and promulgate the true interpretation."[21] Thus they were in agreement with the Psalm writers and the Prophets who stressed the evils of sacrifice.

We read that on all holy days, in fact, upon all occasions where, according to Leviticus, sacrifices of animals were to be given, the Essenes gave as their sacrifice an "humble and contrite heart."

They claimed to have had access to the pure law of Thanksgiving as it was first given to Moses before "lying priests and vain scribes" had perverted it to suit their own lusts.

> "I shall hold it as one of the laws
> Engraved of old on the tablets
> To render to God as my tribute
> The blessings of my lips."[22]

Philo of Alexandria, writing during the time that Jesus had his ministry says: "They are called Esseni because of their saintliness. They do not sacrifice animals, regarding a reverent mind as the only true sacrifice."[23] That is, they give themselves as a sacrifice.

Professor Teicher writes: "But we have there (in the Essene scriptures) the emphatic prohibition of eating animals. No consumption of meat means no killing of animals and both together mean no sacrifices of animals."[24]

What was the attitude of the Palestinian followers of Jesus regarding animal sacrifice?

In an original "Aramaic Matthew" used by the Nazarenes, Jesus says, according to Epiphanius (XXX16),

"I am come to abolish the sacrifices, and if you do not cease from sacrificing, the wrath of God will not cease from you."

Apparently this saying did not survive the Greek translation, probably because it inferred that God disapproved of the lack of mercy shown his creatures.

However, a similar inference apparently did survive translation. In Matt. 12:7, Jesus says: "If you know what this means, I desire mercy instead of sacrifice, you would not condemn the innocent." Here Jesus quoted Hos. 6:6: "I desire mercy instead of sacrifice, the knowledge of God more than burnt offerings."

In Acts 6:14, Jesus is accused of changing the customs which the priests and scribes attributed to Moses. Apparently the custom referred to here was that of the sacrifice, for Stephen, to whom the charge was directed, answered by quoting Prophet Amos: "Did you offer me slain beasts and sacrifices forty years in the wilderness, O House of Israel?" (7:42).

In Hebrews we read: "Let us offer the sacrifice of praise to God, that is, the fruit of our lips giving thanks to His name," (13:15) or as the Dead Sea Scrolls impart: "Render to God as my tribute the blessings of my lips." [25]

From an Epistle of Barnabas, the companion of St. Paul, we read: "For He made it plain to us through all the prophets that He desires neither sacrifices nor burnt offerings. A heart that glorifies its maker is a fragrant odor to the Lord." [26]

Many other illustrations could be offered to support the case at hand, but the reader will probably agree that further proof is unnecessary.

Here on this point alone, the custom of animal sacrifice, we find a unanimity of agreement among a singular people of Palestine—singular because they were the only people in their part of the world who did not adhere to the general practice of animal sacrifice.

We now consider point (6) which refers to the practice of Vegetarianism.

This is an issue which the Church down through the centuries has employed every means at its disposal to either discredit, obscure, or compromise. However, it is the purpose of this writer to seek out and to reveal the evidences of truth regarding the customs and practices of the early Church, even though such testimony might pose a challenge to the moral and spiritual completeness of modern day Christian teaching. Here, again, the writer's intent is not to criticize, but rather to enlighten.

There is no more positive means of determining the oneness of identity of those called Essenes and those whom tradition refers to as Palestinian Christians than to expose their common rejection of the otherwise universal practice of slaughtering animals for food.

As the prophets had cried out against the evils of the feast days with their sacrifices, the Essenes did likewise, for their scriptures say: "But as for Thy people, lying priests flatter them and deceitful scribes lead them astray. They have plotted wickedness seeking to exchange Thy holy engraven word for the smooth things they address to Thy people, making them turn their gaze into the errors they teach, revel in their feasts, ensnaring themselves with lusts." [27] *

Again, from the Essene scriptures we read: "Let not a man make himself abominable with any living creature or creeping thing by eating of them." [28]

Epiphanius, a bishop during the third century, wrote: "The Essenes eschewed the flesh of animals." Josephus says the same, but in a more subtle manner: . . . . "they all sit down together to one sort of food." [29]

---

* Old Testament writers describe the desire to eat flesh as a "wanton craving," or a "lusting."

He further states that they "live the same kind of life as those whom the Greeks call Pythagoreans." [30] Voltaire writes: "It is well known that Pythagoras embraced the humane doctrine of anti-flesh eating. There was a rivalry as to who could be the most virtuous—Essenes or Pythagoreans." [31]

Josephus says: "They live the longest lives, many of them exist above a hundred years, owing to the simplicity of their diet." [32] Porphyry also referred to their repast as a "single simple dish of pure, clean food." [33]

St. Jerome expressed admiration for the Essenes: "those who perpetually abstained from meat and wine and had acquired the habit of every-day fasting. That habit, it is true, is attested by the Therapeutae, whose connection with the Essenes cannot be doubted." [34]

There are evidences that the cave in which the earlier discoveries of the Scrolls were made, had been entered during Roman times. Both Professor Harding and Father De Vaux attest to this. [35]

"In a letter composed . . . . about 819 C. E. Timotheus relates that Jews from Jerusalem, seeking admission to the Church, had told him that about ten years before. . . . a cave was discovered near Jericho containing a hoard of Hebrew manuscripts of the Bible and other writings, and that these were taken by Jews to Jerusalem.

"The Rabbanites in Jerusalem adopted religious practices that were not at all customary among Talmudic Jewry. They became partly vegetarians, at least to the extent of not consuming meat of oxen and sheep.

"We must conclude that the Rabbanites and the Karaites unexpectedly discovered these writings and that the shock of the discovery was so great as to revolutionize their whole religious outlook.

"Actually, vegetarianism, the dietary restrictions . . . derive from Zadokite writings (Qumran Scriptures) and both the Karaites and the Rabbanites appear to have borrowed these customs from the same source." [36]

And now one might ask: "From where and through whose influence did the sect called Essenes derive their vegetarian practices?"

Various scholars have recognized in the doctrines and the way of life of the Brotherhood a remarkable resemblance to Buddhistic and Pythagorean teachings.

This same influence is also to be noted in the preaching of Jesus. "The ethical system of Buddhism reappears substantially unaltered in the Gospel of Jesus," [37] writes a well-known scholar who proceeds to set forth the many almost exact parallels.

However, aside from Buddhistic and Pythagorean influences, it is quite obvious that the food reform practiced by the Brotherhood was mostly influenced by many references in the traditional Hebrew Scriptures which oppose the killing of animals either for sacrifice or for food. A review of these might be somewhat of a shock to the average Christian or Jew who has not recognized their inner meaning, as, no doubt, did the Holy Ones at Qumran.

However, the intent of the writer is to seek out and to interpret what the evidence seems to justify as the truth, opinions to the contrary notwithstanding.

But before recalling a few of these references, which still appear in our traditional Scriptures though somewhat softened in tone, it should be noted again that the Essenes claimed to have possession of the pure Law of Moses as it existed before it had been perverted by false scribes and lying priests. [38]

Therefore, in accord with Essene teachings, if this Law did not call for the sacrifice of animals then it must also have prohibited the slaughter of animals for food, for usually the two went hand in hand, as the Prophets so forcefully remind us. "Put your burnt offerings into sacrifices and eat flesh," cried Jeremiah, "for these things I did not command of your fathers. Walk only in the way I command, that it may be well with you." (Jer. 7:21-23). "They love sacrifice, they sacrifice flesh and eat it, but the Lord has no delight in them." (Hos. 8:13 R.S.V.).

Titus Flavius Clemens, one of the most learned of the early Christian fathers, wrote: "Sacrifices were invented by men as a pretext for eating flesh." [39]

Apparently the prophets, long before the Essenes, had access to the original law of Moses, for they were the first to denounce the false expositors. (Gaster.)

"Trust ye not in lying words, saying, the temple of the Lord are these," cried Jeremiah (7:4). "The Prophets prophesy falsely and the priests rule at their direction and my people love to have it so." (5:31).

"How can you say we are wise and the law of the Lord is with us. Behold! the false pen of the scribes has made it into a lie." (Jer. 8:8).

During the Persian period, the original story of Creation was attributed to Moses. No doubt later renditions of it were recognized by the Prophets as the work of "lying Priests," for certainly the phrase wherein God is described as "pleased" with Abel's burnt offering of the lamb, could not possibly have escaped their condemnation.

Indeed, the prophets, the Psalm writers, and many of the other scribes in more or less positive utterances condemned either or both, the killing of animals for sacrifice and the eating of flesh.

Apparently the text which particularly impressed the Qumran Priests and influenced their doctrine of abstinence was the dietary ordinance set down by the great "Lawgiver." (Gen. 1:29). Being the first reference in the scriptures concerning diet, it is indeed unprecedented, a fact of which the "Holy Ones" must have made special note.

Having complete faith in the infallibility of their God, they could not conceive of Him as making faulty ordinances, or admit His word to be as changeable and willynilly as that of man. They, therefore, considered His prime ordinance as it is written to be the one great truth. "Behold, I have given you every herb-bearing seed and every plant which is upon the face of all the earth, and every tree with fruit yielding seed; for you they shall be for food." (Gen. 1:29).

Evidence that the Essenes gave special attention to this ordinance is witnessed by their own scriptures, wherein we read:

"Thou has created plants for the services of man, and all things that spring from the earth, that he may be fed in abundance; and to them who acknowledge Thy truth, Thou hast given insight to divine Thy wondrous works, and to tell forth Thy knowledge."[40]

The author of this text was no doubt deeply impressed by the wisdom of Daniel, who refused the king's meat and partook only of "those things that spring from the earth." "And God gave Daniel wisdom and understanding to divine all visions and dreams. . . . Gave him insight to divine his wondrous works and to tell forth his knowledge." (Dan. 1:8-17).

This brings up another point which must have no doubt deeply impressed those among the Elect who, as Josephus reports, "took great pains in studying the Scripture that they might choose out of them what is most for the advantage of their soul and body."

As has been witnessed by their own Scriptures, the Essenes obeyed the diet ordinance set down in Gen. 1:29. Obviously what impressed them most was the fact, according to Genesis, that when God gave man the plants, the green herbs and the fruits of the trees for food, He did so with His *blessings*. ("And God saw what He made, and behold, it was very good.") But on the other hand, when flesh meat was added to the diet of man it was obviously given with a *curse*: "For now the fear of you and the dread of you shall be upon every beast and even the hand of man will your blood be required." (Gen. 9:2,3,5)

Apparently the Essenes chose to remain within the good graces of their God and quite obediently sought to conform to His blessings rather than to His curses.

It is quite obvious, according to the Essene doctrines, wherein the original Law of Moses prohibited the sacrifice of animals, and also as set forth in Gen. 1:29 prohibiting the eating of flesh, that the sixth commandment, "Thou shalt not kill" applied to animals and humans alike.

Indeed, one can very well suppose that the Essenes considered both the sixth commandment and the dietary formula of Gen. 1:29 to be companion ordinances, whereby one supplements, facilitates, or confirms the authority of the other.

According to the evidence, it appears that Isaiah was the favorite prophet of the Essenes. The same might also be said about Jesus, for He too quoted freely from Isaiah.

Returning to the commandment, "Thou shalt not kill," we find in the Book of Isaiah a text which apparently confirms the universality of this sixth commandment: "He who slaughters an ox is like him who kills a man." (66:3). The texts continue by comparing the sacrifice of a lamb to the killing of one's dog, and sums up by declaring: "they did what was evil in my eyes, and chose that in which I did not delight." (66:4).

Again, in Ecclesiastes the sacrifice of animals is referred to as evil: "Guard your steps when you go to the House of God: to draw near to listen is better than to offer the sacrifice of fools, for they do not know they are doing *evil.*" (5:1).

According to the scriptures, this same God, through His Prophets, not only denounced the ritual of the sacrifice but He deplored the shedding of the blood of His creatures: for example, in Isaiah: "To what purpose is the multitude of your sacrifices to me, saith the Lord. I delight not in the blood of bullocks or lambs, or of goats. Who has required this at your hand? Your appointed feasts my soul hateth. I will hide mine eyes from you: Yea, when you make many prayers I will hear not, your hands are full of blood. Wash you, make you clean, cease to do *evil.*" (1:11-16).

Here again, the practice of sacrificing animals is referred to as "doing evil." Psalm 26 also refers to the same: "I will wash mine hands in innocence so will I compass thine altar . . . gather not my soul with sinners, nor my life with bloody men, in whose hand is mischief."

Again Isaiah stresses that it is evil to slay oxen, to kill sheep and to eat flesh: that this iniquity can be purged only by death. (22:13,14). In other words, according to Isaiah, one reaps what one sows.

Apparently the Essenes, who fostered an intense belief in the immortality of the soul, took special note of these words of Isaiah, as evidenced by their ascetic ideals through which they carefully avoided all practices which the scriptures condemned.

However, aside from the sixth commandment and the dietary ordinance of Gen. 1:29, the Prophet Isaiah was not the sect's only sustaining influence. Many other Scriptural references, even as we have them today, both support and verify the stand taken by the Essenes. From their own scriptures we read: "Show mercy to your neighbors, and have compassion toward all, not toward men only, but also toward beasts." [41] And from Proverbs we read: "A righteous man regards the life of the beast: but the mercies of the wicked are cruel. He that tilleth the soil shall be satisfied with bread, but he who follows vain persons (the works of vain scribes) is void of understanding." (12:10,11).

"Rescue those who are being taken away to death; hold back those who are stumbling to the slaughter.

"If you say, 'Behold, we did not know this,' does not he who weighs the heart perceive it? and will he not requite man according to his works? My son, eat honey, for it is good and know that wisdom is such to your soul." (Prov. 24:11-14)

"Be not among winebibbers, among gluttonous eaters of flesh, for the drunkard and the glutton will become destitute." (Prov. 23:30, 21).

"Woe to those who stretch themselves upon their couches and eat lambs from the flock and calves from the midst of the stall. They shall be the first to be exiled." (Amos 6:4-7).

Certainly the Essenes must have noted in the Psalms where the disregard for the diet formula of Genesis 1:29 is referred to as a "wanton craving."

"So He saved them and delivered them from the power of the enemy . . . But they soon forgat His works, they did not wait for His counsel. But had a wanton craving in the wilderness . . . and God gave them what they asked, and sent a wasting disease among them." (Ps. 106:R.S.V.) In other words, according to Numbers, "ere the flesh was between their teeth the Lord smote the people with a very great plague. And He called the place Kibroth-hattaavah: because there they buried the people that lusted." (11:33,34)

Would not the prophets of Qumran have interpreted this reference as reflecting the curse which embellished the inclusion of flesh for food? (Gen. 9:2,3,5). It certainly appears that they did, for apparently not a few of the many references pertaining to both the killing of animals either for sacrifice or for food as set forth in the Scriptures were overlooked in the forming of Essene doctrine on the subject. No doubt the scriptures handed down to us through centuries of questionable translation and expedient editing were even more revealing on the subject when the Sect called Essenes apparently recognized in them the authority for their ascetic practices.

Apparently their aversion to animal sacrifice and the eating of flesh was the result of a careful analysis of what appealed to them in the Scriptures as the most honorable, the most dignified, the most merciful and as therefore the most truly Godly.

Here we apparently find the answer as to where and through whose influence the Sect of the Scrolls acquired and practiced a fleshless dietetics.

We now consider the subject according to our information on the practices of those given the traditional name "Palestinian Christians."

"The first Church of Jesus came into existence in Jerusalem. We know that it baptized, celebrated the Eucharist .... We have every reason to believe that they insisted on ... vegetarianism. In short, the new communion was patterned upon the Essene." [42]

The celebrated church father Epiphanius (315-402) said: "The Sect of the Nazarenes dwelt in the Decapolis near Pella . . . all the apostles settled in Pella after the removal from Jerusalem in consequence of Christ's injunction to leave the city and emigrate in view of the impending siege." [43]

As we have noted before, the name Nazarene comes in part from the Oriental word *Nasara* which is *Messianist*, a name given to those whom Philo later called "Essenoi."

Again, as was noted before, the Sect of the Scrolls were known as the "poor" which, in Hebrew is *Ebionim*. Thus, those called the Ebionites and the Nazarenes were actually one and the same. *

"The Ebionites were a party of Jewish Christians who saw in Jesus a man on whom the Spirit descended at his baptism to fit Him for His mission. In practice they were vegetarians, looking with abhorrence on flesh as food and the slaying of animals for sacrifice." [44]

---

*See "Ebionite" (Encyp. Britt.)

Jerome found the Nazarenes also dwelling in Peraea beyond Jordan, (Decapolis or Pella) and classed them with the Ebionites.

"Origen says that these Jews who have received Jesus Christ were all called by the name 'Ebionites'"; [45] (*Viz. the poor*). "What Origen reveals here is that these Jews are the original children of the New Covenant and are direct followers of the Nazarene Jew, Jesus Christ, and His Apostles, thereby conforming devotedly to the practices and customs taught by the Master." [46] This is substantially verified by St. Epiphanius (C. 350) who writes that "the Ebionite Sect (sect of the poor) was in existence (35 CE)," [47] which connects them with the time of Jesus.

The most revealing of all our evidence regarding the true way of life of Jesus and His Apostles is contained in what some scholars believe to be the original gospel, "the gospel according to the Hebrews." This name, however, cannot have been original, for the Hebrews themselves would not have used this designation. It may have been known simply as 'the gospel'; the language was western Aramaic, the mother tongue of Jesus and His Apostles." [48] It was regarded by many in the first century as the Hebrew original of the canonical Matthew (Jerome in Matt. XLII-13: Adv. Pelag III,1). It circulated among the Nazarenes (Ebionites) beyond Jordan. Parts of it appear in the canonical Matthew and other parts of Luke, which suggests that this was the original gospel from which the New Testament versions were taken.

The Gospel of the Hebrews, or the 'Gospel' as used by the Nazarenes, was called "The authentic Matthew," according to Hegesippus, (A.D. 160).

"Eusebius, like Origen, implies that many reckon it canonical, while Jewish Christians make use of this gospel and take small account of the others." [49]

"Of some thirty fragments extant, Nichelson regards ten as independent of the canonical Gospels. Handman thinks that twelve are nearest to St. Luke, eleven to St. Matthew, and six to St. Mark. Lessing (1784), the first to realize the importance of the Gospel of the Hebrews, finds here the original 'Hebrew Matthew' mentioned by Papias in A.D. 110, and the primal source of all the other synoptic Gospels." [50]

According to Hastings Encyclopedia on Religion and Ethics: "The Gospel according to the Apostles was used by the Ebionites (viz., Nazarenes). Herein is found the 'Essene Christ.' He denounces sacrifice and the eating of flesh. Jerome identifies this Gospel with the Gospel of the Hebrews. Lipsuis accepts the statement of Jerome and is of the opinion that this gospel in the form in which it was known to Epiphanius, Jerome, and Origen—was a copy of an older original written in Aramaic." [51]

Again from a responsible source, we read: "They, (Ebionites, viz., Nazarenes) read from a gospel written first person, Matthew being the spokesman in the singular, and the Twelve Apostles speaking in the plural. This led to its being called, especially by Epiphanius, by such names as, According to Matthew, the Gospel of the Hebrews, Gospel of the Twelve, and the Gospel of the Ebionites.

This gospel, which is the same original Matthew we are discussing, "describes the food of John the Baptist as wild honey and cakes made with oil and honey. The Greek work for oil cake is 'enkris,' and the Greek word for locust is 'akris.' [52]

It is understandable how these words could have been confused in copying, purposely or otherwise. In fact, St. Jerome writes: "We must confess that as we have this gospel in our own language, it is marked by discrepancies." [53]

As we have noted before, Epiphanius tells us that all the Apostles settled in Pella *(Peraea)* along with the Nazarenes (viz., Ebionites). This is to say that these people were in direct fellowship with the Apostles of Jesus, in which case they abstained from wine and the flesh of animals, because they were instructed to do so by the Apostles themselves.

Our documentation tells us that "they followed the Apostles in their custom of daily lustrations. They refused to partake of flesh or wine, taking as their pattern, St. Peter, whose food was bread, olives and herbs." (Hoer 15:cf. Clem. Hom.XII,6) [54]

We learn from the Church Father Eusebius, quoting Hegesippus (about 160 A.D.) that James, the Lord's brother,—drank no wine nor ate the flesh of animals. Also, an early century Christian document, "presents Thomas as fasting, wearing a single (probably white) garment, giving what he has to others, and abstaining from the eating of flesh and the drinking of wine." [55]

Clement of Alexandria reports that "Matthew lived upon seeds and nuts, fruits and vegetables without the use of flesh." (Clem. Instructor).

According to the Gospel of John, two of the Baptist's disciples followed Jesus. One of these was Andrew; the other may have been Jude who was also from Bethsaida. Andrew was Peter's brother, both in the flesh and in the faith. He would therefore conform to the same way of life as did Peter. Also, he and the other disciple, whom we have called Jude, were disciples of the Baptist who practiced and no doubt preached the virtues of a humane diet. We cannot therefore consider them to be other than abstainers from animal food.

That it was paramount to the qualification of a disciple that he abide by the Gen. 1:29 precedent is indicated in the choosing of Matthias to fill the place in the twelve vacated by Judas, (Acts 1:21-26), for his food was the same as told of Matthew as in the writings of the great church Father, Clement of Alexandria. [56] According to these historical records, one can safely hold that the other apostles of which little is known, also ate of an innocent table in accord with the teachings of their Lord.

147

According to the Scriptures, St. Peter went out of Peraea, and preached in Bithynia. There he taught the knowledge of Jesus Christ, for records tell us that his followers adhered strictly to a "harmless," or "innocent" diet.

Pliny, who was the Governor of Bithynia where Peter had preached the Gospel of Jesus, wrote a letter to Trajan, the Roman Emperor, describing the early Christian practices: "They affirmed the whole of their guilt, or their error; they met on a day before it was light (before sunrise) and addressed a form of prayer to Christ as to a divinity, binding themselves by a solemn oath never to commit any sin or evil and never to falsify their word, nor deny a trust, after which it was their custom to depart and to meet together again to take food, but ordinary and harmless* food." [57]

It is quite obvious that this is an Essene-Christian custom. Josephus writes of the Essenes: "They assemble before sun-rising and speak not a word about profane matters, but put up certain prayers . . . . after this every one of them is sent away . . . . then they assemble again . . . . and sit down together each one to a single plate of one sort of food"; [58] i.e., harmless or innocent food.

Pliny referred to Christianity as a contagious superstition, describing those under suspicion as abstaining from flesh food.

Seneca, some forty years earlier, referred to those under imperial suspicion as: "the foreign cultus or superstition who abstained from the flesh of animals." [59]

Many of the early Christian fathers, including the saints, adhered strictly to a humane diet. In fact, many of them were quite vehement in their denunciation of flesh eating.

---

* Some translators use here the word" harmless"; others the word "innocent." Both refer to food that had suffered no harm or hurt, viz., blood guiltless.

The great Christian Father Flavius Clement, the founder of the Alexandrian School of Christian Theology, succeeding Pantaenus (A.D. 190) wrote: "It is good neither to drink wine nor to eat flesh, as both St. Paul * and the Pythagoreans acknowledge, for this is rather characteristic to a beast, and the fumes arising from them (the fleshpots) being dense, darken the soul. . . .For a voice will whisper to him (Paul) saying: 'Destroy not the work of God for the sake of food.' 'Whether ye eat or drink, do all to the glory of God,' aiming after true frugality. 'For it is lawful for me to partake of all things, yet all things are not expedient. For those who do all that is lawful quickly fall into doing what is unlawful.' For just as righteousness is not attained by avarice, nor temperance by excess, so neither is the regimen of a Christian formed by indulgence, for the table of truth is far from lasciviousness.

"Nor are you in the midst of the repast, to exhibit yourselves hugging your food like wild beasts nor helping yourselves to a fullness of sauce, for man is not by nature a gravy eater, but a bread eater." [60]

Clement continues: "It is far better to be happy than to have a devil dwelling in us, for happiness is found only in the practice of virtue. Accordingly, the Apostle Matthew lived upon seeds, grains, nuts and vegetables, without the use of flesh." [61]

The writings of St. Chrysostom, the most eloquent of the Christian fathers, are most voluminous on the subject. He says: "No streams of blood are among them (those who abstain), no dainty cookery, no heaviness of head. Nor are there horrible smells of flesh-meats among them, or disagreeable fumes from the kitchen. . . .With their repast of fruits and vegetables, even angels from Heaven, as they behold it, are delighted and pleased." [62]

---

* Clement apparently infers that St. Paul, as did the old apostles, abstained from flesh food.

"In the early days of Christianity there was a record which was valued very much, in which the pure Christian . . .the Jewish ideas on the subject were debated. I refer to the Clementine Homilies, which date back to the middle of the Second Century. This record was founded on the preaching of Peter and in it we have these words: 'The unnatural eating of flesh is as polluting as the heathen worship of devils, with its sacrifices and impure feasts, through participation in which a man becomes a fellow-eater with devils.'" (Homily XII.) [63]

The great figure in Latin Christianity was Florens Tertullian. He was born in Carthage about 155 A.D.

Cyprian, the Bishop of Carthage, referred to him as the "Master," suggesting that Tertullian had firsthand access to the wisdom of Jesus himself. Tertullian writes: "How unworthy do you press the example of Christ as having come eating and drinking into the service of your lusts— He who pronounced not the full, but the hungry and thirsty blessed, who professed his work to be the completion of his Father's will, was wont to abstain—instructing them to labor for that food which lasts to eternal life, and enjoining in their common prayers, petition not for flesh food but for bread only." [64]

The knowledge that was Tertullian's is indeed sustained by a fragment of the writings of the Apostolic Father Papias. (c. 60-125).

This fragment was preserved by Irenaeus (second century). It describes John as quoting Jesus as follows: "A grain of wheat will produce ten thousand heads, and every head will have ten thousand grains, and every grain will produce ten pounds of fine clean flour. And other seeds, fruits and grass will produce in corresponding proportions, and all the animals will use those foods that are products of the soil and become in turn peaceable and in harmony with one another, and with man." [65]

150

Here speaks "The one whom the Gentiles seek," according to Isaiah 11:6-7. Through knowledge of him, "the leopard shall lie down with the kid, and the cow and the bear shall feed their young ones together"; i.e., as "using those foods that are products of the soil," in accord with Gen. 1:29,30.

These sayings are purely allegorical, but the message they convey is unmistakably clear. No one but an abstainer who abhors the very thought of one creature destroying another for food could have spoken them.

Thus we conclude our discussion of what clearly appears to be the most convincing of all the evidences concerning the singleness of identity of the Sect called Essenes and the sect tradition referred to as Primitive Christians. In fact, there was only one sect of people in the whole of Palestine, or in the areas round about whose food was vegetarian. Call them what you will—Essenes, Nazarenes, Ebionites, or Primitive Christians, for these are merely names which are for the most part alien means of describing or identifying a singular people, a people whom Pliny referred to as "strange above all others in the entire world."[66]

We conclude this study of the several proofs of relationship with a discussion of Point 7, the doctrine of nonviolence as opposed to war.

"Now as to those called Essenes, they were known as the 'Sons of Peace.'

"For all who walk by the counsels of the Spirit, the visitation consists of healing and abundant peace throughout their days." (DSD).

Philo of Alexandria writes about the Sect: "As for darts, javelins, daggers, or the helmet, breastplate or shield, you could not find a single manufacturer of them nor, in general, any person making weapons or engines or plying any industry concerned with war; not, indeed, any of the peaceful kind which easily lapse into vice." [67] As to the latter,

151

Philo probably refers to knives which people use for butchering.

Josephus writes: "They dispense with anger after a just manner, and restrain their passion. They are eminent for fidelity, and are the 'ministers of peace.'" [68]

The Essenes were the only sect of their time in Judaism who abhorred war and the soldier's calling.

And now as to New Testament reports in reference to Christianity. First in Luke, the soldiers address John the Baptist, asking "'And what shall we do?' And he said unto them, 'Do violence to no man . . . '" (3:14). This is to say, "put aside your weapons and seek your profession in the ways of peace."

Jesus, in the Sermon on the Mount, in speaking of those whom Josephus referred to as 'ministers of peace' said: "Blessed are the peacemakers (the pacifists) for they shall be called the children of God." (Matt. 5:9). And in the same breath, he stressed His concern for these same children of God: "Blessed are they which are persecuted for righteousness sake, for theirs is the Kingdom of Heaven." (Matt. 5:10). Well he knew the plight of the conscientious objector who was to persevere as a "Child of God."

"In concrete and vivid precepts, the Sermon on the Mount sets forth the character and conduct of those who really follow Jesus, of those who may really be called God's children, of those who shall submit to the rule of God, of those who shall enter His Kingdom; in short, of true Christians: the pure in heart, the meek, the peacemakers, those who hunger and thirst after righteousness, and are willing to suffer for its sake. They are the salt of the earth and the light of the world. And then follow the commandments: 'Ye shall keep yourselves from murder but also from revenge. And in place of an eye for an eye and a tooth for a tooth, resist not that which is evil, but whosoever smiteth thee on thy right cheek, turn to him the other also.' Can one find one little implication in these words that does not plead for peace or that does not shrink from violence in every degree or form?

"Jesus does not give detached commands. He brings your whole being and doing and suffering under the compulsion of one single principle. 'Ye have heard that it was said, Thou shalt love thy neighbor and hate thine enemy, but I say unto you: love your enemies, do good to them that hate you, bless them that curse you, pray for them that despitefully use you and persecute you, that ye may be sons of your Father which is in heaven.' (Matt. 5:43-45, Luke 6:27-38). Love even your enemy! This is the highest demand that can ever be made. *This love of enemy is not just one virtue among many, but the fairest flower of all human conduct.*

"It is indeed the greatest, for while faith and hope are scarcely attributes of God, He loves with an eternal love; *God is Love. (I John 4:8). Therefore, the children of God can be like the Son only by so loving.*

"It is recognized that these commands, though they lay stress on the inward disposition and have not the force of law, were certainly meant as concrete instructions for the followers of Jesus. They had to be obeyed. Their carrying out was counted on. Behind these injunctions, which admit no cleavage between conduct and character, stands the newly sent Ambassador of God, with His 'But I say unto you.'

"Not only the war of aggression but also defensive warfare is ruled out by the Sermon on the Mount. . . .The gospel condemns war. . . .We have primarily to recognize, however hard it may be to do so, that the waging of war has no place in the moral and spiritual teachings of Jesus." [69]

"Hippolytus, second century Christian Father and historian, put down in writing what he believed to be the Apostolic tradition and so the authentic Christian (Essene, Nazarene, Ebionite) teaching. He maintained that when a

153

soldier applied for admission to the Christian fellowship, he must refuse to kill men, even if he were commanded by his superiors to do so, and also must not take an oath." [70]

Justin Martyr, the principal apologist of the early Church (c. A.D. 150) writes that: "Christians seek no earthly realm, but a heavenly, and this will be a realm of peace. The prophecy of Isaiah—that swords shall be beaten into plowshares and spears to pruning hooks—begins to find fulfillment in the missions of Christians. For we refrain from the making of war on our enemies, but gladly go to death for Christ's sake. Christians are warriors of a different world, peaceful fighters. For Caesar's soldiers possess nothing which they can lose more precious than their life, while our love goes out to that eternal life which God will give." [71]

St. Paul surely taught that Christian warfare is spiritual, as did the Essenes. Theirs was a war of "the sons of light against the sons of darkness, against the army of Belial. Wickedness will thus be humbled and left without remnant and no survivor shall remain of the Sons of Darkness. Streaks of lightning will flash from one end of the world to the other, growing even brighter until the era of darkness is brought utterly to an end. Then in the era of God His exalted grandeur will give light forevermore, shedding on all the Sons of Light peace and blessing, gladness and length of days." [72]

Origen, the great Christian Father of the second century, would hear nothing of earthly military service; he regarded it as wholly forbidden. "We Christians no longer take up sword against nation, nor do we learn war any more, having become children of peace (namely, Essenes, 'Ministers of Peace') * for the sake of Jesus who is our leader. We do not serve as soldiers under the Emperor, even though he requires it. Persons who possess authority

---

* Parenthesis by Author.

to kill, or soldiers, should not kill at all, even when it is commanded of them. Everyone who receives a distinctive leading position, or a magisterial power, and does not clothe himself in the weaponlessness which is becoming to the Gospel, should be separated from the flock." [73]

The early Christian Father Tertullian (A.D. 200) was a conscientious follower of the "Humane Christ." "He deplored violence in any form, whether applied to man or to any of God's creatures. No Christian writer of ancient times so vigorously opposed militarism as did this eager apologist who was himself the son of a military officer. There is no sense, he said, in arguing about the question how a soldier should conduct himself, what he may do, and what he may not do. We must first inquire whether military service is proper at all for Christians. What sense is there in discussing the merely accidental, when that on which it rests is to be condemned? Do we believe it lawful for a human oath to be super-added to one divine, and for a man to come under promise to another master after Christ? Shall it be held lawful to make an occupation of the sword, when the Lord proclaims that he who uses the sword shall perish by the sword? And shall the Son of Peace take part in battle when it does not become Him to even sue at law?

"The question Tertullian faces is not whether a Christian may be a soldier, but even whether a soldier may be allowed within the church. He answers 'No.' The soldier who becomes Christian ought to leave the army. There is no agreement between the divine and the human sacramentum (oath), the standard of Christ and the standard of the devil, the camp of light and the camp of darkness. One soul cannot be true to two lords—God and Caesar. How shall a Christian man wage war; nay, how shall he even be a soldier in peacetime, without the sword, which the Lord has taken away?—for in disarming Peter he ungirded every soldier." [74]

155

The great Church Father Cyprian, Bishop of Carthage, out of reverence for Tertullian, read daily from the Master's writing. As a Christian preacher, he, of course, utterly repudiated war and wrote: "The whole earth is drenched in adversaries' blood, and if murder is committed, privately it is a crime, but if it happens with State authority, courage is the name for it—not the goodness of the cause, but the greatness of the cruelty makes the abominations blameless. Christians are not allowed to kill; it is not permitted the guiltless to put even the guilty to death." [75] (Harnack).

The Christian writer Lactantius of Bithynia writes on the Sixth Commandment: "When God prohibits killing, he not only forbids us to commit brigandage, which is not allowed even by public laws, but he warns us not to do even those things which are legal among men. And so it will not be lawful for a just man to serve as a soldier, for justice itself is his military service, nor to accuse anyone of a capital offense, because it makes no difference whether they kill with a sword or with a word, since killing itself is forbidden." [76]

"Erasmus, a fifteenth century Christian Father, scholar and theologian, regarded it a sacrilege for a warrior to stitch the cross on his standard. 'The cross,' said he, 'is the banner and standard of Him who has overcome and triumphed, not by fighting and slaying, but by his own bitter death. With the cross do ye deprive the life of your brother, whose life was rescued by the cross?

'O, you cruel, shameless lips; how dare ye call Father whilst ye rob your brother of Life?

'Hallowed be Thy name'—how can the name of God be more dishonored than by war?

'Thy kingdom come'—will ye pray thus while ye fight at nought and shrink from no bloodshed, however great?

'Thy will be done on earth as it is in heaven'—God desires peace and ye make war.

'Ye pray your common Father for daily bread, and meantime ye burn all your brother's rye and corn.

'How shamefully will ye say—'Forgive us our trespasses as we forgive them who trespass against us,' while ye desire nothing else but to slay and to do mischief.

'Ye pray that ye may not come into danger or temptation and ye lead your brother into every sort of danger and temptation." [77]

Many more references could be added to this list of admonitions which come from the pens of some of the most eminent Christian authorities.

However, it is not the purpose of this writer to challenge the Christians' sincerity, or to question the manner in which he approaches his allegiance to Christ, or as to how or why he regards the master's teachings.

These are his own individual affairs or responsibilities, from, or through which he alone may find "peace of mind," (the only true security), or suffer the consequences of his lesser judgment.

And so, again, the purpose of this writer was merely to discuss the seven points pertaining to the beliefs, customs and practices of certain people—to set these up as evidences to prove, not the mere similarity, but the actual singularity, of those given, or called by, names such as Essenoi, Essenes, Nazarenes, Ebionites, and Palestinian Christians. In other words, to distinguish in no uncertain terms the common relationship of a people whom it now seems proper to identify as "Esseno-Christians."

CHAPTER NINE

References

[1] Walker, Roy, *The Golden Feast*, Macmillan, N.Y. Taken from Porphyry's treatise, Jane Harrison's *Study of Greek Religion*.

[1a, 52] Goodspeed, Dr. Edgar, *History of Early Christianity*, University Press, Chicago

[2, 6, 9, 23, 67] Philo of Alexandria, *Quod Omnis Probus Liber* (c. A.D. 20).

[3, 5, 8, 29, 32, 58, 68] Josephus, *Wars of the Jews*, Book II, VIII, 3-13.

[10, 18, 30] *Antiquities*, Book XVIII, Chap 1, 5, B. XV, Chap. X, 4.

[4, 17, 19, 21, 22, 25, 27, 38, 40, 72] Gaster, Theodore H., *The Dead Sea Scriptures*, Doubleday & Co., N.Y.

[7, 66] Pliny the Elder (c. 70 A.D.) *Historica Naturalis*, Book V, Chap 17.

[11] Dupont-Sommer, A., *The Dead Sea Scrolls*, Basil Blackwell, Oxford, McMillan, N.Y.

[12, 13, 15, 46] Ewing, Upton Clary, *The Essene Christ* (out of print).

[14] Latourette, Kenneth Scott, *The History of Christianity*, Harper, N.Y.

[16] Davies, A. Powell, *Dead Sea Scrolls*, Signet Key Book

[20] Brownlee, Dr. William H., *Bulletin of the American Schools of Oriental Research*, 1951

[24] Teicher, J. L., *Journal of Jewish Studies*, 1954

[26, 65] Goodspeed, J. Edgar, *The Apostolic Fathers*, Harper & Brothers, N.Y.

[28] Burrows, Millar, *The Dead Sea Scrolls*, Viking Press, N.Y.

[31, 33, 39, 61, 62, 64] Williams, Howard, *Ethics of Diet*, Albert Broadbent, Manchester; Richard J. James, London.

[34] Vermes, Geza, *Discovery in the Judean Desert*, Desclee Co, N.Y., Paris, Rome.

[35] Biblical Archaeologist, Dec. 1950.

[36, 43, 47] Teicher, J. L., *Journal of Jewish Studies*, 1951

[37, 42] Larson, Martin A., *The Story of Christian Origins*, published by the author.

[41] *The Twelve Patriarchs*, (Zeb. 2:1), World Publishing Co., N.Y.

[44] Findlay, Rev. Adam, M.A., D.D., *The Apocryphal Gospels from the History of Christianity in the Light of Modern Knowledge*, Harcourt & Brace, N.Y.

[45, 49, 50, 51, 54] Hastings Encyclopedia on Religion and Ethics (V. 5, p. 143), Charles Scribner's, Sons, N.Y.

[48, 56] *Encyclopedia Brittannica*, Vol. 2, p. 180, 11th Ed. Vol XVII, p. 895.

[55] Bartlett, James Vernon, M.A., The Apocryphal Gospels from the *History of Christianity in the Light of Modern Knowledge*.

[57] Pliny The Younger, (*Gainus Plinus Secondus*, 53-110 A.D.). Governor of Bithynia under the Roman Emperor Trojan.

[59] Seneca's letter to Lucilius, Howard Williams, *Ethics of Diet*.

[60] Clement of Alexandria (c. 150-220) (from *The Instructor*), Anne Fremantle, *A Treasury of Early Christianity*, a Mentor Book.

[53] *Ibid*, Letter from Jerome to Pope Damascus.

[63] Ferrier, Rev. J. Todd, *On Behalf of the Creatures*, The Order of the Cross, 10 Devere Gardens, Kensington, London.

[69, 70, 71, 73, 74, 75, 76, 77] Heering, Prof. G. J., *The Fall of Christianity*, Fellowship Publications, N.Y.

CHAPTER TEN

Some New Insights into the Purpose of Jesus and the Little-known Facts Concerning His Crucifixion

In the preceding chapter, we reviewed certain texts taken from Scripture which may well have provided the foundation for the ethical system practiced by the "Sect of the Scrolls." These, as has been shown, opposed generally and in some instances most emphatically the custom of slaying animals, whether for food or for the ritual of sacrifice.

In complete accord with the Prophets' pleas for mercy instead of sacrifice, the Sect believed that one should *slay the beast within,* rather than slay an innocent creature to affect atonement for the earth.

In other words, they gave of themselves through renouncing as evil the carnal customs which made jest of the love of God for all his creation. One must first seek the Kingdom of God through bringing his own soul into harmony with his mercy-loving will. Thus, a Covenant of Justice replaces the sacrifice of the blood of the lamb and a *redemption through compassion* "insures requital of the wicked."

Here the Essene scriptures provide fresh insights into the idea of giving of one's self in sacrifice—an idea that expanded to become the greatest living example of self-giving the pen of man has ever recorded.

Here, also, in response to all the supporting data, a new light is shed upon the purpose of Jesus—a light so infinitely pure that it shines far beyond the vain pretenses of a self-indulgent society.

In an early record of events, called *According to the Apostles*, a text used by the "poor," the "meek," and the "elect" followers of James, the Lord's brother, and the old Apostles, Jesus denounces the sacrifice of animals and the eating of flesh. [1] Again, in the original Aramaic Matthew, a gospel used by these same "blood of the fathers kin to the Master brethren," the purpose of Jesus was to abrogate the sacrifice. He declares: "If you do not cease to sacrifice, the wrath of God will not cease from you." [2]

Again, in the New Testament recension of the Aramaic Matthew, Jesus stresses on two different occasions his aversion to the merciless custom of animal sacrifice. He challenges the Pharisees by saying: "If you know what this means, 'I desire mercy instead of sacrifice,' you would not condemn the innocent.' (Matt. 12:7, 9:13). Here Jesus quotes from the prophets he had vowed to fulfill. (Matt. 5:17). "I desire mercy instead of sacrifice, the knowledge of God more than burnt offerings." (Hosea 6:6). "He has showed you, O man, what is good, and what the Lord requires of you, but to do justice and to love kindness" is Micah's rebuke to the practice of animal sacrifice. (6:6-8).

"O Lord, open thou my lips and my mouth shall show forth thy praise. For thou hast no delight in sacrifice. The sacrifice acceptable to God is a humble spirit; a meek and contrite heart, O God, thou wilt not despise." (Ps. 51:15-17).

"Though ye offer me burnt offerings and your meat offerings, I will not accept them; neither will I regard the peace offerings of your fat beasts. Have ye offered unto me sacrifices and offerings in the wilderness forty years, O house of Israel?" (Amos, 5:1, 22, 25.)

Thus the most appealing, as well as the most urgent protests of the Prophets were directed toward the custom of sacrifice. They wrote and they preached all manner of tirades concerning this affront to God, but alas! their pleas had little or no effect on the temple authorities. Only a soul-stirring exhibition of the most daring and sensational nature could awaken the people and bring about a victory for the cause of righteousness. This Jesus was well aware of when he made plans to cleanse the temple.

"Sacrifices and offerings thou didst not desire; mine ears hast thou opened. Lo, I come; in the volume of the book it is written of me. I delight to do the will of my Father; Yea, His Law is within my heart." (Psalm 40).

It was but a few days before the Passover that Jesus said to His disciples: "Behold, we go up to Jerusalem and all things that are written by the Prophets concerning the Son of Man shall be accomplished." (Luke 18:31).

"In Him shall be fulfilled the prophecy of Heaven concerning the Lamb of God. . . .He shall enter into the temple and thereafter be treated with outrage, and He shall be lifted up upon a tree." [3]* (Essene Scriptures parallel with Luke 18:32,33).

That Jesus had forecast His death to His disciples indicates that He had carefully planned a course of action, the consequences of which would be inevitable. Well He knew that He would sign his own death warrant the very moment that He dared to demonstrate against the gods of Rome, for in denouncing the Pharisees' custom of slaying animals for sacrifice, He would automatically denounce the temple rites of Rome.

---

*From Scriptures used by the "Sect of the Scrolls."

All this leads up to what appears to be the most significant of proofs regarding the offense which demanded the extreme penalty from Jesus, and why any charge supposedly placed against Him by the Sanhedrin is trivial in comparison. In Jesus' day, Judea was a Roman province shaped to fit the measure of Roman laws and to a particular extent certain religious customs and practices.

The temple at Jerusalem was rebuilt by the gentile Herod the Great with the support and the blessings of imperial Rome. Its priesthood officiated in certain rites which were sacred to both the Pharisees and the Romans.

The inner temple was the exclusive *beth elohim*—"Holy of Holies" of the priests, but the outer portals of courts were not so restricted. Here stood the great stone altar upon which sacrifices were made to Yahweh. Here, too, the priests received and offered the sacrifices of Caesar.

Under Roman rule one courted certain death if he dared to demonstrate in any manner against the custom of animal sacrifice. This is a fact not generally known, and for which reason the gospels lay stress upon the money changers as being the object of the temple cleansing, even though, as the gospel of John admits, the sheep, oxen and the doves were the victims of the practice.

It was in the Roman courts of the temple area where Jesus denounced those who changed denarii for shekels, who bought, sold and traded various articles of value so that the sinner might obtain, according to his means, a sparrow or two, a couple of doves, a lamb, kid or other victim to be offered up in the bloody ritual of sacrifice.

According to Josephus: "Eleazar, son of Ananias, the high priest, a very bold youth, who was at that time governor of the temple, persuaded those that officiated in the divine service to receive no sacrifice for any foreigner. And this was the true beginning of our war with the Romans, (c. 42-70, A.D.) for they rejected the sacrifice of Caesar on this account; and when many of the high priests and principal men besought them not to omit the sacrifice which was customary for them to offer for their princes, they would not be prevailed upon." [4]

Conforming to the reports of Josephus, if it were an offense *equal to an act of war* for the Jews to reject the custom of receiving the sacrifices of Caesar, then most certainly anyone guilty of rejecting or demonstrating in any manner against the temple sacrifice was also guilty of a demonstration against Caesar. Thus, in his act of cleansing the temple, Jesus committed a manifold crime against the authority and the pride of imperial Rome, as well as against her gods.

Therefore, let it be made clear that the gospel reports have purposely been made to confuse and to make light of the temple incident, first (as was mentioned before) by a centering of the incident on the money changers and again by misplacing its continuity in reference to the Passover and the crucifixion, and last, but not least, by obscuring the fact that the Romans* and not the Jews caused the arrest, the conviction and the crucifixion of Jesus.

Returning to the purpose of Jesus we find Him hurriedly leaving the temple, along with His disciples and making His way to a secret place in the desert.

It was necessary now that He remain in hiding until the appointed time. The die had been cast; there was no turning back; no possible way to escape His fate even if He had desired to do so. He was now a marked man and it was only a question of when and where the Roman authorities would find Him and condemn Him to death.

To this end was Jesus committed, for the Essene Scriptures say "a sinless one shall die for the ungodly men in the blood of the covenant" [5] —namely, the blood of the lambs slaughtered for the Passover. In conformity here-

---

* A more complete study of the condemnation of Jesus is found in this author's book *The Essene Christ* (at present out of print).

with, Jesus' final act is seen as having a far greater moral and spiritual significance than that of a mere protest against the temple ritual as such. Indeed, had not God through His prophets denounced the custom, and pleaded for lovingkindness instead of sacrifice? Likewise, was not Jesus also to denounce the temple ritual because of the wanton cruelty, the torture, pain and death inflicted on these innocent creatures? How else can one interpret the word *mercy* in reference to the sacrifice and the knowledge of God? (Hosea 6:6).

Mercy is asked by God in consideration of His creatures. Mercy and lovingkindness instead of pain, suffering and death.

Thus, in Jesus, the pleading voice of a God of all creation spoke through the voice of God in the flesh of man and the greatest humane act in the history of the world became a fact of record. Supreme it was because it involved the giving up of his own body to the same torture and death as that inflicted upon a hundred thousand Paschal lambs.

This Jesus knew long before he went forward in His final soul-stirring mission to *fulfill* the Prophets. Many times before He had succored man from his cares and pains, but now His boundless love and compassion reached out toward the innocent creatures of God's kingdom, for they, too, knew pain and suffering; they, too, were from the same life-giving bosom of the Father of all Creation.

The Agony in the Garden

"Then He went out and His disciples followed him to the Mount of Olives. He withdrew from them a little way and kneeled down to pray." (Luke 22:39-41).

The agony in the Garden of Gethsemane can best be understood as a deep, compassionate concern for the inevitable suffering of all life, as a tender reaching out toward a million homes and firesides, yea, toward a thousand hills, gathering together into itself all the heartaches, pains and sufferings endured therein. Indeed, it can better be understood as a deep subjective awareness of all the harm, hurt and sorrows awaiting all creatures, and an overflowing pity for the waywardness of human understanding.

Without the least concern for his own welfare, the agony of Jesus is again more meaningfully explained as the frustration of an infinite love, crying out solicitously for the salvation of all the living.

That beautiful prophecy of Isaiah: "The wolf shall lie down with the lamb" must have brought tears of "blood to the master's cheeks as He knelt beneath the symbolic branch of the olive." "The leopard shall lie down with the kid and no creature shall hurt nor destroy upon all my holy mountain, for the earth shall have full knowledge of the Lord as the waters cover the sea." (Isaiah 11).

Was not this prophecy spoken of Him and had He not failed to fulfill its objective?

Was He an innocent victim of the toils of some strange paradox?

One wonders if questions or realizations such as these did not represent the bitter cup which Jesus prayed to have taken away. Certainly in His own nature He was Himself the very essence of Isaiah's prophetic vision, but He could only strive for peace and speak out against the evils of the world. He could not bring love and mercy into the hearts of men if they were not ready to receive it, but He could and would gather into His own forgiving self all the pain and suffering their sins caused, and as witness thereof pour the terrible total out through his own tortured flesh upon the cross.

Thus Jesus felt secure in accepting His own appointed destiny, for only in the fulfillment thereof could He hope to convince the people that He and the Father were one, that the concern of God was His concern, that God's love and mercy for all His creation was His love and mercy for all creation. "Believe me that I am in the Father and the Father in me." (John 14:11).

As noted before, the brethren of the Scrolls gave of their inner selves as a sacrifice to God for the salvation of the earth. But Jesus gave not only of His inner self but His flesh and blood also—yea, even His very life for the salvation of the world and the requital of the wicked.

This was the great sacrifice whereby humanity might recognize the enormity of its crimes against the God of all life: that man's awareness of the death of an innocent Christ would remind him of his responsibility to other innocents of God's creation, that through his remorse might come mercy, and from mercy lovingkindness and through lovingkindness, full and complete understanding.

"Think, then," pleads the venerable Cardinal Newman, "of your feelings at cruelty practiced upon brute animals, and you will gain one sort of feeling which the history of Christ's cross and passion ought to excite within you. And let me add, this is in all cases one good use to which you may turn any. . .wanton and unfeeling acts shown toward the. . .animals; let them remind you as a picture of Christ's suffering. He who was higher than the angels, deigned to humble Himself even to the state of the brute creation." [6]

Thus the purpose of Jesus is found to be far more extensive, far more merciful, humane and therefore far more "God-like" than the average Christian is aware of and, shall we say, cares to admit. Indeed, there are still those who want to feel that their ability to call "Christ! Christ!" is strictly their own personal passkey to Heaven and that the Saviour has no ear for the unvoiced.

The true meaning of the sacrifice of Jesus, the intent behind the giving of himself for the salvation of all creatures, has not been lost. On down through the centuries, His unfailing concern for all that has (consciously or otherwise), touched the hearts of people of every faith and every calling. Some were and are scholars, some clergymen, theologians, teachers, mystics, poets, artists and writers, geniuses in their chosen fields. Some have been elevated to the celestial realms of sainthood, while others without fanfare or exhortation of any kind have witnessed the prophetic vision being brought to pass in their own quiet way of life. But these last are not the least. Even though their praises are unsung among men, they in their humble reverence for all life and for their God are indeed equal to the greatest among the saints.

CHAPTER TEN

References

[1] *Hastings' Encyclopedia of Religion and Ethics*, Charles Scribner's, Sons, N.Y.

[2] Epiphanius, (XXX,16) Probably from the Aramaic Matthew, the gospel used by the Nazarenes or Ebionites.

[3, 5] *The Twelve Patriarchs* (Ben. 2:7, 1:21), *Lost Books of the Bible*, World Pub. Co., N.Y.

[4] Quote from Josephus (*Wars*, Book II, Chap. XVII, 2).

[6] Agius, Dom Ambrose, O.S.B., *Cruelty to Animals*, London Catholic Truth Society.

"And He shall open the gates of Paradise, and give to the saints to eat from THE TREE OF LIFE, and the spirit of holiness shall be upon them."
    —*The Testimony of the Twelve Patriarchs* (Levi)

- -

Another book in this field published by TREE OF LIFE PUBLICATIONS:

The Unknown Life of Jesus Christ, by Nicolas Notovitch. Translation of an ancient manuscript found in a lamasery in Tibet. One answer to the question: "Where was Jesus during the 18 'lost years' not mentioned in the Bible?"

Index

"Books that Heal and Inspire"

*   *   *   *   *   *   *

Tree of Life Publications

P.O. Box 126

Joshua Tree, CA 92252

CHARGE ORDERS: (800) 200-2046
BOOKLISTS AVAILABLE
FAX: 760-366-3596; PHONE: 366-3695